I WOULDN'T DIE

A Memoir

Enjoy the journey into my life.

2005

I WOULDN'T DIE

A Memoir

By
FRANCO ANTONETTI

Vīa Novī Press

Cover and text design by Ital Art
Photos: from the personal collection of Franco Antonetti

If you are unable to order this book from your
local bookseller, you may order directly from the publisher:

Via Novi Press
P.O. Box 2091
Gilbert, Arizona USA 85299-2091
www.francoantonetti.com

ISBN 97-80970-91122
10 9 8 7 6 5 4 3 2 1
Printed in Canada.

Dedication

For Coach Russ Hunchar

Contents

Introduction

I am writing about a young boy who came so close to losing his life so many times that it seems a miracle he is alive at all. And he is alive. Let me explain.

First, the poor child was buried alive as a baby. But he survived—by time and chance and God's grace—but also because he *simply would not die.*

The second time was a bicycle accident that would have killed anyone else, but, as I was saying, this boy would not die.

And then the worst of all possible mishaps. The boy's own brother, welcoming him home from the hospital, dropped him accidentally, and cracked his skull on the front steps of the family apartment.

Shortly after this, the boy, who was wiser now—or thought so, anyway—swam across a river and ended up battling for his life in a swamp of quicksand. He was saved by a couple of lovers hiding in the reeds. A helping hand dragged him out of the mire.

Each time, the boy survived, he lived–but for what reason, he wondered. Why was he always so close to dying and yet always spared, as if in the hands of an angel? Angels, he believed in, and saints and magic and many other things besides.

So, after a while, he began to realize he was blessed. And so he walked on window ledges high above the city to prove he would not fall. And if he did, to prove that no matter what, he would not die. All this happened in Rome more than fifty years ago, but it seems to me, today, to be only yesterday. Well, anyway, when the boy was ten years old he went to the United States with his pants legs stuffed with sausages.

And thus the accident-prone boy from Italy who would not die grew into a man in America, and faced a whole new series of challenges, as well as more encounters with the grim reaper. Anyway, I have to say now . . . I am that boy, I am that man. The things that have made my life—a friend's outstretched hand, a coach who took the time to advise me on the importance of an education, and the mysterious way in which I survived so many life-threatening situations—these are all the things that make life worth living. Not just dodging bombs and hiding in caves and coming out unscarred, but the little gestures of the human heart. The saving grace of friends, often people you do not even know.

So this is the story of the boy who wouldn't die and the man who, not dying, lived a life different from anyone else on earth.

I ought to know. It's my life.

Franco Antonetti
Gilbert, Arizona
2003

Rome, Italy

Chapter One

The behind-the-scenes action of any war is not noticeable by most people because they are not personally affected. It is hard for them to comprehend what famine is really like unless they have experienced it for themselves. Loss of a life is, of course, the most tragic experience that each individual must deal with. Franco who was to be born in mid-July of 1944 in Rome, Italy, would join an older sister Maria and a second sister who was originally called Maria but whose nickname, Ofelia, reduced the confusion. Franco would also join a brother Aldo who was born some nine years earlier and under much better circumstances. There was also a younger sister named Chriseide.

Chriseide was quickly given to her aunt since it was almost impossible to feed that many children in such difficult times. The aunt lived quite far from Rome in a little town in the southern part of Italy called Lucera. I am told that this was a common practice in those times, although I do not think I could ever give up a child of mine under any circumstances.

My mother, no doubt, had a difficult life, and unless you were actually there, it is not possible to imagine how she made such a decision nor how she made ends meet for the rest of the family. She had a very close girl friend named Annita and possibly they gave each other the strength to endure the horrifying experiences that they shared for a number of years.

Prior to my birth my mother had a number of pregnancies that were terminated by her friend and she, in turn, assisted her in the same manner. The unborn were a burden—but so were the born. I was the burden in July of 1944 and my mother's friend attempted to abort my birth. In her own unusual and cruel way, however, she was not able to do it successfully. And thus I emerged into a devastated city on July 17th. Not unlike the many children before me, I was born in a bathtub. Brought into the world by the same midwife who had also tried earlier to end my life. Such are friends. And such are the times of war.

In any case, I survived the first death and came into life healthy.

A terrible famine followed my appearance.

One morning my mother and her friend decided that if they were to survive the war, they must go farther south where there were farmers and also work on farms.

So my mother Raffaella and her girlfriend Annita took my brother Aldo, my two sisters Maria and Maria-Ofelia to the train station to hitch a ride southbound. I was three months old at the time this trip began. The train itself was an old coal-powered one and it was under heavy allied fire at the time. My mother Annita and the children sneaked on the back of one of the cars.

Now Italy has many mountains, as you are certainly aware. The Alps to the north divide France, Germany and Austria. In the central part of Italy there are more mountains running from north to south. Train tracks ran right alongside the mountain ranges and some of the tracks went right through the heart of them. As we were going south, we did exactly that—went straight through the mountain tunnels which were deep and long.

A few hours into our journey, the tunnels became more frequent and the belching smoke from the coal-driven engine made all of us cough. One of the final tunnels was so long that it caused my face to turn blue. Apparently, I had stopped breathing.

Finally, we came out of the tunnel. It was apparent to both Raffaella and Annita that God had answered their request in a strange way. Franco, who was such a burden on these two poor women, was on his way to heaven.

Chapter Two

As the train approached a small village, the women instructed the children how to jump just before the train came to a halt. This way they would have a better chance to get away, in case a conductor or some other authority should see them. Once off the train, there was the problem of explaining to the children what had happened to their younger brother, and then the additional problem of what to do with the body.

Annita and Raffaella realized the best thing to do was to bury Franco in a hurry, hopefully jump back on the train, and get to the next stop where they could begin to search for food. They bent to the task, digging with their hands. Finally, using the back of a shoe and a stick found near the tracks, the two women got the shallow grave done. Franco was laid to rest in a hole that barely covered his forehead. The children looked on in silence. Suddenly, the jolt of placing Franco down on his back brought out a faint cry that caused the children to gasp and cry out, "He's alive!"

To this day, I am not sure if this was accepted as good news.

My being dead must have been a tremendous load off my mother's mind. One less mouth to feed, one less thing to carry and worry about. She would once again have free hands to assist in the work that was to come. At the same time my mother looked at Annita and whispered, "Somehow I had a feeling that from the beginning when the abortion failed, this boy was special and he wouldn't die." Annita nodded. She, too, felt the same way.

And that was how Franco was lifted from his first—but not his last—grave. There were more to come, but he, in his innocence, could not have known about anything except the air that was back in his lungs and the dirt that was hurriedly brushed off his face.

After leaving the train at the next stop, my mother and Annita found a cave near a farm. There they were able to live and work in exchange for produce and leftovers.

There were many times when the family saw fighter planes drop low and fire away at our people who had to run and hide to protect themselves. Although my brother Aldo was inside the cave when this happened, the experience left him with an eye-twitch that is still there sixty years later. I, of course, have no memory of the strafe planes except the stories that are told sparingly at family get-togethers.

Once the war ended we returned to Rome where my mother and Annita shared an apartment. I remember it quite well, and as a matter of fact, I recently visited Rome to see if indeed it was still there. Via Novi numero14 still stands and our apartment number 10 looks as it did in my recollection of nearly fifty years ago. I spent a great deal of my life there with very little supervision. My mother and father separated (divorce was not an option in Italy at that time) and she worked many hours at various jobs to keep us fed and the bills paid.

One of her jobs was scrubbing the marble steps of the four-story apartment building. She also worked at the local movie house cleaning after the shows. Her final income was from a chiosco, a little store. This was really a four-foot-by-five-foot shed that was situated twenty-minutes away by means of tranvia, an Italian trolley car. Items my mother sold there were mostly soft drinks like Coke and Italian ice that we planed off an ice block that my mother bought daily. Upon the customer's selection of syrup, my mother sprinkled it on the ice in a paper cup. As time went on she also sold pumpkin seeds and slices of coconut.

Chapter Three

My next denial of death came when my brother decided to take me for a walk. I was about eighteen-months old. We were walking from our little courtyard toward the Giuseppe Garibaldi School that I would attend in a few years. We were but a few steps from the school when a young man sped by on a Bianchi bike. He came too close, and striking me in the middle of my head, my skull split wide open.

The bicyclist kept on going. I'm sure he was scared of what he had done. Aldo panicked. He stood there watching me bleed and listened to me scream. Here was another time in my life when my future was in someone's hands other than mine.

A woman saw the accident, and without batting an eye she picked me up in her arms covering herself with my blood, and ran to the nearby Catholic Hospital.

The doctors used clamps to hold the head wound together and to stop the bleeding. I remained in their care for weeks, but my survival was thought to be only hopeful.

My mother did not find out about the accident until she saw my brother crying in front of the gates to our apartment building. When she spoke to him, he had no idea where I was. "I killed him," he exclaimed. "I killed Franco!"

Of course, he did have some of the blood on him and naturally my mother was confused when she heard his story. Her first thought, however, was to rush to the hospital with my brother. Once there, she got a better version of the story.

The woman who really saved my life did not return. To this day I do not know who she is, but I hope one day to meet her. Stranger things have certainly happened. In fact many of them happened to me, as you shall see.

So the nurses told my mom what a strong and courageous boy I was, and how close everyone had come to losing me. Once again my mother wondered about me. But she told the nurses, "This boy is different, I can tell you that. Worse things have happened to him, but he wouldn't die."

The day came at last when I could leave the hospital.

By then all the nurses knew me and liked me a lot and whenever they had a chance to show someone "the miracle child" they did. They ran their hands through my hair and showed off the huge gash that was there. "You see, nothing stops him from smiling," they said. It was true. I smiled all the time. I still do.

After a small celebration, we returned to our apartment at Via Novi.

My brother could not say sorry enough and he blamed himself for the accident. He was very happy to see me at home, so happy that he hoisted me to his shoulders, and began to climb the three stories of marble steps that went up to apartment 10.

Somehow he lost his balance, fell backwards and dropped me on my head.

We were back at that hospital within thirty minutes of leaving it.

No one at the hospital could believe it. They could not imagine such a thing could happen twice to such a small child.

Naturally my mother was all nerves.

Aldo started blinking like a camera shutter at a racetrack.

I did not know any of this, as I was unconscious, but later people told me.

It must have been God—how else can you explain that I was still alive? Anyway, at this moment one of the nurses looked at my mother and said, "He will not die."

This time the hospital stay was quite long and the healing process very slow. Once again, I managed to survive. But even today you can put your fingers on my head and feel the crack in my skull.

Chapter Four

My days as a student would begin at the tender age of five by getting into our designated uniform for school that was fortunately only at the end of our street.

The school was like a fortress as it had walls all around and once you entered through the front gate all activities were within this compound. The boys wore blue smocks the length of a dress and the girls wore white smocks of the same length. School was simply business; general studies and that was all. We did not have the luxury of study period, wood shop, metal shop or recess. If we did not pay attention we were paddled. Naturally we did not want our parents to know if we got into trouble, because that meant additional paddling at home. In my case, I could always talk my way out of it. At the early age of six I realized that I was different from most of my classmates. I had ideas and a will to make them known. Early on, I was a talker. And now I learned that talking could get you into, and out of, trouble. Both ways, I was good with words, and I used them often.

At this time it became clear to me that two factors governed my life: food and money. There was never enough of either one. We had a little store in front of our home and it was owned and operated by a nice old man named Carlo. Each day I would pass Carlo's store on my way to school as well as on my way back, and I saw a lot of scrap paper being handled in there. One day I asked Carlo if I could help out with the paper work. Carlo knew who I was. "Sure, you can help a little if you like."

Basically, he had to separate all of these second hand office papers that he collected from all over the city. I had the job of taking out the carbon paper that was in the random piles at his store. Then the papers had to be stacked according to size and weight. I did this for one or two hours every day. Carlo gave me fifty, sometimes a hundred *lire*. At that time, a movie cost fifty *lire*, so it was pretty good money. I also saw a great deal of tobacco in boxes at Carlo's shop.

He told me, "You know, the kids collect cigarette butts and I nip off the filter part, as well as the paper holding the tobacco and I place the used tobacco in a large box and we sell it."

Hearing this, I immediately got an idea. I decided to go the *tranvia* stops where I knew people smoked while waiting for the trolley. Often they would pitch the half-smoked cigarette as the trolley pulled up to the stop. So, the first day I heard about this, I brought Carlo a good collection of cigarette butts, and to my surprise I had two hundred *lire* worth. To me this was much better than separating papers and breathing in all that office dust and carbon smell.

I also experienced another way of making money at the tranvia stations. One day as I waited at one of the stops, a nice lady asked, "Little boy, are you lost?"

I said, "No, I'm not lost. But I haven't got any money for the ride home."

The lady replied, "Oh, you poor dear."

Then, giving me one hundred *lire*, she said, "Be careful, little one."

She departed on the next trolley.

"Well, that was easy," I told myself.

After that I took my book bag filled with books, and started crying at the stop to make my predicament even more dramatic. Whenever anyone saw me, man or woman, I got a positive response, and some money. The generosity of these people was incredible.

After giving me a couple hundred *lire*, my benefactor always asked, "Is this the trolley you take?"

"No, I take number 18," I said making sure the number was different than the one at the stop. I also made sure to work alternate stops, as well as times, so I'd get assistance from people who had not seen me before.

So for the first time in my life I was not hungry all the time.

Chapter Five

I was now buying chocolate bars at the same market where I got olive oil for my mother. I filled a liter bottle, our own, by cranking a handle, and the storeowner marked it on a piece of paper for my mother to pay at a later time. However, the chocolate bars and chestnuts that I got were paid for with the cash I had earned myself.

One day the owner talked to my mother about all the stuff I was buying on a regular basis and she got furious.

"What do you mean? He can't afford to buy such luxuries!"

"Oh," the man said, "your little boy pays for anything he buys for himself."

That afternoon when I came home, my mother was waiting for me. She sat me down hard and said, "I hear you're buying chocolate. Where is all this money coming from?"

"I earn it working for signore Carlo."

She glared at me. "How can that old man let a six-year-old work under such conditions? I'm going to let him have it."

"Oh, please don't," I begged. "Don't be upset with signore Carlo. He's such a nice man and if it wasn't for him, I'd be more hungry than I am right now."

She cried hearing that. Then she went on to tell me how important it was for me not to get into any trouble. If I did, she said, I could not go to America.

"If you have a record you will be rejected and this will keep the entire family from going."

My mother's father, Grandpa Joe, was living in the United States. He had left my mother when she was a little girl to find a better future for the family, and now he was asking all of us to come and join him.

"The paperwork was filed in 1947," my mother explained. "It takes a number of years to get approved, but you must be healthy and not have a criminal record of any kind."

Now I started to think about some of the things that I did that could have gotten me in real trouble. Certainly the trolley deal was not exactly honest, but from my point of view, it was not bad enough to get me prosecuted. However, I had done another scheme that was more aggressive. I had a buddy named Mario who was about six months younger than me and we made a little wooden box with a cross on it and a slot on top for collecting coins or paper money. Mario and I would jump up behind a moving trolley, and hang on to the hoses that coupled the cars.

We would use this method for various reasons.

The main reason was to get from one place to another. But also to get there at no cost. We hitched a trolley to areas where no one recognized us. Then we visited tall apartment houses where there might be as many as one hundred families living in them.

We went door-to-door collecting funds for San Giovanni Church. This was a very large church that everyone knew about, and in most cases people were proud to see little boys doing such nice work at such a young age.

Every so often someone said, "May I know your mothers' names and addresses, please?" And we answered with false names and made up fake addresses, and they never doubted a word we said because we said it so sincerely.

So the box was full in no time. And Mario and I had as much money in one afternoon as my mother made in a whole week.

It is funny how some minds work. I remember the first time we came back from one of our collection days. We got off at a stop near our home. As we neared the huge white statue of Mary that is just off the New Appian Way, we stopped.

It was hard to walk by her without looking. She was made of marble and her eyes stared at us no matter where we were. We would walk, and look, and her eyes were always on us. Mary saw us coming, she saw us in front of her, as well as when we were going by her, and those penetrating eyes of Mary followed me to sleep sometimes.

Anyway, that day that Mario and I stopped and looked, we both got the same idea. We decided that if we shared some of the money with Mary, it would all be OK.

At the base of her feet there was a slot for donations.

We were generous and gave her five hundred *lire.*

What a relief that was. Probably more for me than Mario. Because, at that time, with all the things running through my mind in regards to America, I had to be extra careful with my money-making ideas.

Another thing we used to do for fun, which could have gotten us in trouble was going to the *Colosseo,* and playing there for hours. In 1950 the Coliseum was open and no one was there to charge you for a visit.

We used to go on the Old Appian Way, too. There we climbed trees and collected pinecones. These were the ones that bear nuts. Mario and I would dry them for weeks and once dry, we would open them up, and harvest the *pignoli* and sell them to the old ladies that worked the corners selling hot chestnuts, pumpkin seeds and such. Many times after collecting pignoli, we went to play in the catacombs and scare ourselves until we were chased away by guards, or worse, the *Carabinieri,* the Italian police.

Another of our hangouts was a place called Marana, a small river that runs in Rome. We used it mostly to swim and watch the skinny dippers, guys with their girlfriends, but we also used the river for an escape route. We went to a certain farmer's field and helped ourselves to fruits and vegetables, after which we swam across the Marana so the farmer could not catch us.

The river was not always such a gracious savior. It was known to take the lives of the unwary. In some places there was quicksand. One day I was running full speed to get away from a farmer. I had taken a dozen ripe tomatoes. They were so good; I ate six or seven.

Then I took some more with me for the way home, and that was when the farmer spotted me. He started shooting at me. I was told later that it was rock salt, but then I was flying and he was shooting, and I did not look back.

I dived into the river losing the few tomatoes I had. Swimming hard, I reached the other side, a distance of about seventy-five feet. As I started to run out of the river, I felt myself unable to move. I struggled. I was sinking with each step.

By this time the angry farmer had turned back and I was alone. I was sinking fast.

I asked myself, "Is this how I am going to die with a mouth full of mud?"

Then I heard some giggling nearby. In the canes that were plentiful along the river this laughter just bubbled up, and then I saw a young half-dressed couple. They popped their heads out of the canes and saw my struggle.

I was still sinking when the young man offered me his hand. Then he started to sink. My heart pounding, I watched helplessly as he backed away.

Now I was up to my chest in quicksand, and I was terrified.

"*Aiuto!*" I yelled, help.

The youth then grabbed a tall cane and ripped it out by its root and pushed it towards me. I lunged for it, took hold. Slowly I pulled myself ever closer to him. At last I was out of the quicksand, gasping for breath.

I'd lost both of my shoes and socks, but I was alive.

I thanked the young man. "You saved my life," I said.

He grinned, "It was nothing."

Then his girl friend gave me a big kiss that I can still feel on my lips. After I took leave of them, I looked back at the river. That day there were no people fishing or sitting on the riverbank. I realized that if the young couple had not been there, I would not be here.

Chapter Six

I have not said very much about my family. The reason is that basically we were all on a free-for-all. As long as no one got into serious trouble, life just moved along as it always did. Our meals were unplanned. When we ate, the fare was predictable.

Polenta, the Italian equivalent of grits or oatmeal, was the usual thing that filled us up.

To spice up the taste, my mother made a meatless tomato sauce and that made the *polenta* taste nice.

There is a family story that is laughable today, but not at the time. It was like this, my mother simply said, "Tonight, children, we're going to have chicken cacciatore."

Since I could count the times we ate meat in our lifetime in Italy, my mother's promise of cacciatore made my mouth water. It made all of our mouths water.

We did not have a refrigerator, and of course, we did not have a television set. In this we were not alone in our neighborhood and so I watched TV by climbing a tree across from a furniture store where there was a set that was on all the time. I sat in that tree watching television until my legs fell asleep.

As for the refrigerator, most people shopped every day; not having a fridge, we never missed it. Bread was a big thing and we had plenty of that and if we did not I went to our local store and charged it. The common sandwich was a thick slice of the hard bread, wetted down with a little sprinkle of water and then some sugar. A better tasting upgrade was to use olive oil instead of water but we did not always have olive oil and we could only charge a liter per month.

When I started making money in my creative ways I often used a chocolate bar between two slices of bread—that was incredible. We also got packages from my grandfather in America.

He lived in a place called Berkeley Heights, New Jersey.

He sent us packages of Pet condensed milk, Colgate toothpaste (that I thought was an Italian brand like Palmolive). I used one can of Pet milk per week, diluting it to make a liter of milk. I put anything stale in a bowl and freshened it up with the milk.

But I see that I have gotten off track and not finished telling about the famous chicken cacciatore. Well, as it happened, my mother came home after work and said the chicken she purchased flew away. "I'm sorry," she said, sighing, "that I cannot make our special meal."

In Italy most homes and apartments have functional shutters made of thick wood with louvers. And in my time, people stored salami, prosciutto, chicken, whatever, on the shutters. The shutters themselves were partially closed and the stored food item was on the inside part that received a fresh breeze. The shutters were like a warm fridge. Of course many times of the year, it was too hot to do this but it was used a great deal when I was growing up, and it still is today.

So—back to the chicken—having had this mouth-watering dinner fly away from me so many times, I vowed to get my own chicken. Very close to our home there was a Catholic Church, school and hospital, as well as a huge enclosed playground.

In this playground you had the most popular soccer field (in Italy it is called *calcione*) and you also had uneven bars, high bar, horse, and climbing poles that would allow you to go as high as twenty feet. There was, in addition, a quarter mile track. I am sure it was in a kilometer measurement, but I do not know what that was.

Anyway, the priests were very good about keeping an eye on the activities and there were plenty of nuns with a huge silver cross hanging from their waist. I got to know the area pretty well. There were windows at grass level showing a floor at a lower level that appeared to be a huge cafeteria for the entire facility.

I spent long periods of time gazing through the windows at Fathers and Sisters eating what always seemed to me to be some type of feast. One day while I was looking at the steaming platters of food, I felt a light touch on my left shoulder. I turned and saw a tiny nun.

"What are you doing?" she asked.

"Just looking."

"This area is not for children."

I said, "But I smell chicken, is that not so?"

"Yes," she replied, "it is so."

I quickly responded that I had not eaten chicken for such a long time, which was perfectly true, and that I just wanted to have a look at it. Hearing that, the little nun encouraged me to elaborate about our family, and I told her the chicken cacciatore tale, and I could see that she was moved, so I laid it on as thick as I could. At the end of my story I managed to squeeze a tear out of my left eye, and that sealed the deal.

Presently the small nun asked me to follow her. "This is a very restricted area," she said. "Only if you are with me or a priest can you enter."

Well, did I eat . . . ..

I had fried chicken, mashed potatoes, carrots, peas and a real glass of cold milk. Once I had finished, the nun asked me, "Do you want a piece of chestnut pie?"

My eyes rolled in my head. Chestnut pie was made from chestnut flour, and it was the best pie in the world. If you like pumpkin pie multiply it one hundred times; it's that good. Now, as it happened, I arranged to visit the little nun every so often—just enough not to ruin my welcome but infrequent enough so she wanted to feed me. I had learned at the tender age of six-going-on-seven how to read people, and, most importantly, when to close a deal.

I had certain ways of making money, too, that I used when other ways needed time to cool off. My father, whom I discovered was not my real dad when I was twelve, worked for the government as a clerk. The rules at his office were quite strict when it came to family visitations and that sort of thing. Knowing this, I would rent a bicycle for the day (it was very common to do that for about five hundred *lire*. At that time six hundred *lire* was equal to a dollar.) So I rode a rented bike to my dad's place of business, a one-way trip of five miles.

At the front desk I asked to see my father.

He would appear shortly, his face livid with anger because government clerks could lose their job for such minor infractions.

"Didn't I tell you the last time that I can't have visitors unless it's a serious emergency?" He stared at me.

"I just need a little money for my bicycle rental," I told him.

His face full of grief and pity, my father shelled out five hundred (and sometimes as much as a one thousand) *lire* just to get rid of me.

Such a visit was well worth it for me, and somehow I doubted he ever got into any trouble, as I was his son, and besides, it was always an emergency.

Since I had plenty of time on the rental, I was not going to waste it on a single mission, so I pedaled all the way to the main train station that went to Ostia, the ocean. This was very close to a pyramid that is in Rome and also not very far from the Coliseum. I had an uncle, Zio Orazio. Well, I was told he was my uncle but in reality he was a friend of the family. As it turned out, though, I learned that he was my real father. In any event, he had a much larger *chiosco* than the one we had.

I stopped just before the bridge where the tiny store could be seen underneath the bridge. If his wife was not around, it was all right to visit him. If she was there, I went elsewhere.

Fortunately for me, this time the coast was clear and I went down to see Zio Orazio.

He was always glad to see me and he gave me an honest hug and a kiss, when I arrived and when I left. Zio made sure I got the best treats, too.

As I was enjoying the candy, he asked, "What about the bike? How much do you owe?"

"I have to pay the rental when I get back."

Zio gave me one thousand *lire.*

If his wife came around the corner, he told me to high tail it, and I did, minus the money. But he always made it up the next time. The story he told me about his wife was that she did not like children. I did not want to start a problem with her, so I believed this for a long time. One of my deepest regrets is that I never told Zio that I loved him, and that I knew he was my father and that I was proud to be his son.

It is so clear to me now whenever I see my brother, five-foot-five, that he is cut just like my dad, same height. So are my sisters, roughly the same height and similar looks. I, on the other hand, am six-foot and look a lot like Zio, who was six-two and weighed 260 pounds.

Chapter Seven

Some of my income as a six-year-old came from gambling. I gambled with the local kids my age and often with boys much older. We had a coin game that went like this. You found a wall of a building and, selecting a coin that you were prepared to lose, say, a twenty-five *lire* coin, you hit the wall with the coin, trying to get it to ricochet as far away from the wall as possible. The player that is playing against you now must take his coin and by hitting the same wall, he tries to get a palm-width away from your coin. If, after coming to a halt, his coin is close enough to yours so that with his palm stretched out he can touch his coin as well as yours, he gets to keep both. If his throw does not come close enough, then you pick up your coin and try to get close to his.

My advantage was that I was much bigger in size than most kids and I also practiced stretching my hand so I would have an inch or two advantage on the other players. I did not win one hundred percent of the time, but maybe a good eighty percent most of the time. Anyway, I made a few hundred *lire* at every game. All this extra money helped me to do things that most kids in our neighborhood could never do.

I started eating specialty items at a regular basis. I went to the movies at the "priests' theater." I took Mario along as my guest. We did this four times a month.

I left the paper-sorting job as well as the cigarette butt job and stuck with working the trolley stops. My dad and uncle were always good, and in a pinch, Mario and I collected for the church.

The things I did then amaze me now. The chances I took. For instance, as I mentioned earlier we lived in a third floor apartment. That building had a six-inch ledge around it. I used to go out our back window and walk the ledge to one of the front windows where I would hop in as if I had come from the sky.

There were other things I did with the window ledge. The window sills in Italy are made of marble. One of my favorite treats was to get some olive oil and place it on the window sill and then pour sugar on it. *Pignoli* (pine nuts) went on top of that. I was making a concoction that was almost like taffy. Clear and hardened, it turned to the consistency of a macaroon. I cut pieces with a knife right on the sill, and ate it while looking down at the people passing below.

Shortly before my tenth birthday, I learned that our emigration papers were finally approved, and that we would be going on a long boat trip to America. We were going to leave from Napoli. Nine days later we would be in the land of dreams. My mother cautioned Aldo and me, "We could still be rejected if you do something stupid, so please be on your best behavior."

So we had to be good for at least the next six months.

My two older sisters were not coming, as each had married and started a family of their own. The eldest Maria had two little girls, Marina and Patrizia. The other Maria had a little boy whose name slips my memory.

I do remember my classmates telling me how lucky I was and how I would forget all about them. I also had a girlfriend who lived on the lower floor of our home and she was sorrowful that I would leave her. Her name was Franca but somehow I was so excited about going to America that leaving her was not that big of a deal. Since I had known about our departure years before, I made sure that we were just happy friends and not more than that.

You wonder how a ten year-old could think like this. But I saw many of my friends get very involved with girls at ages eight and nine and they were having sex on a regular basis by ten. I kissed and did a lot of touching, but I was focused on a bigger picture and nothing was going to take that away from me.

Part of the big picture, for me, was a story I had heard about America. One of my friends said he had heard from his uncle that lying on the sidewalks there were wallets stuffed with money. All you had to do was pick them up and pocket them.

The day finally came. We went to the train station. This wait was followed by the long train ride that seemed to be ten hours but was probably closer to three. Then, after having had shots and going through a bunch of lines we got on an elevator that stopped at seven different levels of the ship. Of course we were way down in a tiny room where my mother was on a bunk at normal level, my brother had a berth above my mother, and I had the highest berth with my nose just about touching the ceiling. I had to resist the urge to sit up as I normally would at home.

We left that afternoon for America.

New Jersey

Chapter Eight

I remember people pointing and saying, "That island out there is Capri." I said to myself, "One day I will return with lots of money, and visit that island of Capri," and I did, but now I am getting ahead of myself. From the deck of our ship, Capri looked rich and beautiful and so clean and so many beautiful boats and ships all around the harbor.

When we passed the Rock of Gibraltar, I looked ahead of the ship and saw porpoises swimming as fast and faster than the ship. This was an unusual experience for me—all the people on the top decks were tourists and most of them spoke English.

I had no clue as to what anyone was saying.

The meals were different, too. I enjoyed them though. It was a luxury for us to eat regular meals and on board ship there were different spices and things we had never heard of, but I tried anything and everything.

As for getting sick from the sea, I had no problem. But when people got sick in stairways where disinfectant was used to sanitize, I got queasy from the smell of the cleanser. There was nothing so chemical-smelling in Italy.

The final day of travel came and we were told that by morning we would be in New York City.

We actually docked outside the harbor that night and docked at Ellis Island at nine in the morning. I saw the Statue of Liberty the first time on December 9, 1954 at about 7:30 AM. She was beautiful and I said to myself that I would touch her someday.

And I have done that many times and climbed inside her great body all the way up to her crown.

Before getting off the ship we had to pack our trunk so that we could go through Ellis Island. I did not know it then, but our group was historic, in that we were the last people to be processed at this famous island. My mother forced me to smuggle about thirty feet of dried Italian sausage. I guess she thought America did not have any, so she brought her own. The sausage must have been given to her by a friend or relative as I never saw it before in our apartment. If I had, I would have eaten a bunch of it.

Anyway, I had to place this long sausage through my shirt, down my pants leg and up the other arm and down the other leg until all of it was hidden. I say, "hidden" but the idea was not well planned. I had trouble walking, let alone trying to look natural.

Actually, I walked as if I had a big load in my pants. As we went up and down the stairs, I was taken out of the line by an inspector. Grabbing me by the arm, he gave a look of surprise. This was not the ordinary arm of a ten year-old, but the bulging bicep of Arnold Schwarzenegger. In no time, the inspector was pulling sausage out of me and another guard came to see what was going on. We attracted a small crowd of guards and they could not believe that the links that kept on coming. Finally they extracted the entire load. My mother did not understand one word that they were saying, but of course she knew that they were going to take it away.

She made a big fuss to no avail and we lost our sausage and I am sure that many individuals enjoyed it, as well they should have.

After what seemed forever we were allowed to start out and my mother suddenly yelled at this old man that I found out was Grandpa Joe, her dad.

Next to him was this little woman, who stood four-foot-nine. Her face looked like a raisin. She was all wrinkly and tiny. But when I looked at her shoes they were the size of a clown's. It is possible she had someone else's shoes on, but they were incredibly big, and that first sight of her huge feet has stayed with me all these years. When we started to leave the building, I saw stairs moving. I saw people on them and they were not moving; yet they were going down.

I ran to the amazing stairs and went up and down at least five times until Grandpa Joe said, *"Andiamo!"*

Grandpa had a 1948 Dodge with fluid drive and a starter that had a button on the floor. The car was large and very soft inside. This was the first time in my life that I was in a car. While I was luxuriating in it and Grandpa was driving us from New York to the little town of Berkeley Heights, New Jersey, I thought once again about the sidewalks full of wallets that I had heard about in Italy.

I asked Grandpa if we could stop for a little while, so I could scoop up some wallets. Grandpa laughed and said, "There's no money in the streets of America, but if you want to work you can make all the money you want." He laughed some more. I said to myself that making it was as good as taking it. That is what I had been doing all along in Italy, but now it was going to be even easier.

Chapter Nine

T he ride to Berkeley Heights was a very long one but to me everything was new and unbelievably exciting. I could not believe the homes that were set all by themselves and with so much land. I could not believe so many little churches and so many bars and I kept asking my grandpa and grandma so many questions that they had to tell me to wait because the questions would be answered in time.

As Grandpa drove along I saw a shopping center for the first time. It took up so much space and the parking lot was filled with huge cars and pickup trucks. I could not remember if I ever saw a pickup truck in Italy. There the most common automobile was the Fiat, known to everyone there as *topolino* or "little mouse."

We finally arrived at what would be my new home. It was a large two-story white house set on a little hill overlooking a big woods on one side and the small town of Berkeley Heights on the other. In back of the house was a very large garden. There were neighbors but not very close, and I thought, "So this is America! Everyone is rich here!" How little I knew at that moment in time. Soon I would learn the truth. But right then, on arriving, I was happy to be living in a dream of my own making.

Grandpa worked for a mason. He was the one who fed bricks and fresh cement to a bricklayer and who set up and moved the scaffolding whenever it was necessary.

There were two other uncles, brothers of my mother, who lived up the street from our home on Garfield Avenue. They were actually stepbrothers. Grandpa had a wife in Italy and she was my mother's mother. But I never met this grandmother because she died giving birth to my mother in 1911. Eight years later in 1919 Grandpa left Italy to find a better life in America. Once in America Grandpa met and married a young lady who owned quite a lot of land in Berkeley Heights. They had two children, my uncle Vito and uncle Joe.

After giving birth to Joe, the second child, my step-grand-mother died from some type of complication. Soon after that Grandpa married for the third time and this woman was the little lady with the big feet who met us in New York. Grandma's maiden name was Suzy Capobianco, which, in Italian, means "whitehead."

Anyhow, Grandpa and Susy had a little boy who died at birth, and that was the last time Grandpa had any other children. As it was, a great number of children and grandchildren carried Grandpa's name, including myself. Well, I had quite a few names and Giuseppe, my grandfather's first name, was in there with the others which, strung all together, were, Gianfranco Emilio Ratamenze Giuseppe Antonetti.

At the time I became a naturalized citizen at age eighteen, I changed my name legally to Franco Antonetti. It was easier that way.

As it was with my uncles, they all had at least one Joe or Joey, Joe-Joe or Junior.

My uncle Vito took over the home that Grandpa used to live in after he built himself a new Cape Cod style house. The old house was a two-story building made of wooden shingles; coal and wood provided heat in the winter.

Our new home was constructed of cinder block and brick. The unusual thing about this house had to do with Grandpa's height. He was five-foot-four and he measured doors and windows according to his height, no one else's. That worked all right for Grandma Suzy, but for growing boys, well, that is another story.

Uncle Vito and Uncle Joe were also laborers. However, Joe had a lot more drive than his brother, and a number of sideline businesses. He had a dump truck that he used to haul trash to the dump for people. He built driveways and did various odd jobs when he was off his regular work.

Vito, on the other hand, was an individual with a heart of gold, who blew his entire paycheck with the guys at a local bar. He worked just enough to get by.

My mother soon found a job in the nearby town Summit. The company was called McGregors and they made clothes. My mother was a seamstress and she did piecework for very little money.

My brother Aldo was almost twenty at this time, and he worked at McGregors, too. He became a presser of suits doing piecework just like my mother.

My job was to go to school.

The local elementary school was Columbia School. It was three to four miles from Grandpa's house, and there were no buses.

My first day at school was, to say the least, challenging.

I had no idea what to wear as all I had was long pants that looked like the kind Payne Stewart used to wear at a golf tournament. The language barrier of course was the most difficult challenge of all. I had no experience with the English language. Worst of all, my grandparents spoke very little English. When they did speak in English, it was slang. So whatever help they gave me was no help at all. For example, I asked my Grandma in Italian, "How should I say to my teacher, 'I want to go to the bathroom'?"

She said, "Tell the teacher you want to go to the *backhouse.*"

"The backhouse?"

She nodded.

Well, I figured she knew.

However, the first time I used that word, my teacher was confused. But since I was dancing and holding my legs together, she understood quickly enough, and I was excused to go to the bathroom.

My luck was with me, though. My fourth grade teacher was an elderly yet totally devoted woman named Mrs. Ross. I owe a great deal to her. She took me under her wing and helped me a lot with everything including my language problem. Many of my classmates were intrigued by this new, awkward, good-looking—so they said—kid from Italy.

I was lucky, too, in that I proved right away that I was good in athletics. In a short time everyone wanted me on their team. One field of study where I looked good was math. The reason was that in Italy we were much further ahead in our school programs. I had learned fourth grade arithmetic the year before and it came to me easily.

Language troubled me, however.

Once we were doing a social studies project where the teacher wanted us to show what made a certain country great or famous, or what products come from that country. We were assigned a map to go with the essay.

When the teacher came to my desk, she said that I could do Italy if I wanted to.

I saw a finished product from a previous class, and it was about France.

That was enough to give the right idea. But I did not understand how the student had made the map of France with mountains elevated from the flat paper and looking so real you wanted to touch them.

The teacher told me that it was easy to do. "Trace a map of Italy," she explained. "Once you've done that, get some flour and water and mix it and make the mountains. When they're dry, paint them."

It sounded easy enough and I ran all the way home being full of excitement. I could not wait to do my project on Italia. I took my time in tracing the main part of Italy, and then Sicilia and finally, Sardinia. I made sure that Corsica was not included as Italy had lost that to France long ago.

Now I had to do the mountains, the Alps, as well as the Appenines.

I asked Grandma about getting flower and water for my project and I also asked if I could continue doing it in the kitchen.

"Go in the back garden," she said. "Pick any flowers you want except the ones from the zucchini, we eat those. We soak them in water and afterwards put the flowers in a batter and fry them."

I told Grandma Suzy that I would be very careful not to step on her plants.

I picked some beautiful flowers and went back to the kitchen and could not wait to show the class my great talent for map making since, in all other things except math and sports, I was lost. Anyway, I used every tool I could imagine to get those flowers to look like a paste but they would not cooperate. The squashed flowers lay on the paper over my tracing and the whole thing was a big mess. I felt stupid. How could I mess up so badly? Had I not followed the directions my teacher gave me?

Finally, I broke down and went to Grandma again.

"These flowers must be the wrong ones or else I don't know what I am doing," I said.

She eyed my map and started to laugh, showing her mouth with most of her teeth missing.

"It's not funny," I protested. "Do you think I want to be a fool in class?"

"I think your teacher must mean the other flower," Grandma Suzy chuckled.

Then she brought out a bowl and some flour and showed me what I was missing. I worked until late in the night and got it done. Maybe it was not as great as I wanted it to be, but I did finish it on time.

School was all-important to me. I knew that I had to learn the language so that I could succeed in America. My classmates took this for granted, speaking easily in the language they were born to speak. But for me it was always difficult and I had to work harder than they did. Fortunately, my athletic prowess counted for a lot. That boosted my self-esteem in a big way. It was a good thing, too. Because no one in my house, including my mother thought school was worthwhile.

Chapter Ten

Grandma, Grandpa, Mother and even my brother thought school was a waste of time. They believed I should be working for the family after school, not playing sports. To tell the truth, I did not have the luxury of living at home for free. The family had decided that I was a wage earner because of my jobs in Italy, and so I was supposed to pay a certain amount each week to cover my living expenses. In addition, I was expected to do most of the household chores that Grandpa said he could not do any longer.

To earn money around Berkeley Heights, I mowed lawns, washed and waxed cars, and when it snowed, I shoveled driveways. I had never seen snow stick to the ground before, but I went out and shoveled sidewalks and driveways and it paid pretty well. I concentrated on the old ladies that I would see on the way to school. I was very polite to them and asked, "Do you want your sidewalk shoveled?" I flashed my best smile, and they always said yes and they not only paid me more than I asked for, but also usually they gave me hot chocolate and a tip.

Uncle Joe added to his income by driving loads of stuff to the dump for people. I helped him one day, and to my surprise, it was a gold mine. I found baby carriage tires, bicycle frames and all kinds of things that I could refurbish. I could actually make a bike from junk parts, paint it, and re-sell it. I made go-carts to order using rebuilt lawnmower engines.

There was a field behind our home that I had to plow with a walk-behind tractor that had a five horsepower Tecumseh engine. The tractor was kept in storage shed, and I added on to it and that was where I stored my bike parts, go-cart parts and anything else I collected. I could not wait to work on these projects of mine, but first I had to weed the garden or plow the field or do endless chores around the house.

The garden was about two hundred feet in width and one hundred feet in length. We planted tomatoes, peppers, green beans and various kinds of zucchini. The tomatoes were time consuming, as we had to pick them, wash them and cook them. Then we had to fill the hundreds of liter bottles that Grandma had in the cellar.

There was a funnel and a thin dowel and you had to drive the dowel up and down until all the tomatoes were gone. I did this until the bottle was nearly full. A basil leaf went in each bottle and I capped it with a stopper. That, too, was done by hand, and it took strength and pressure to do it right.

Once all the bottles were filled (by this time my hands were burning from all the tomato acid) we placed them in a huge tub lined with burlap bags. The metal tub was filled with water and there was a fire underneath it, which brought the water to a boil. The bottles of tomatoes were cooked and cooled and stored in the cellar for future use.

The only thing that seemed stupid to me is that we were storing bottles that we made in 1955 and yet the cellar was full of bottles dating back to 1948. Grandma also had at least eight gallon cans of various oils stored in the cellar. There was also canned milk, sugar, salt, canned fruit and various vegetables.

We also raised pigs, chickens, rabbits, goats, ducks, and turkeys. I got to be friends with all of them especially the pigs. I had no idea how clean pigs were. They always went to the bathroom well away from their sleeping quarters. Grandpa went to the local A & P supermarket and got throw-away items like bad lettuce and other spoiled vegetables, and he brought this home for the pigs. We sunk a bathtub near the shed where they slept and we would fill that tub with water and sometimes spaghetti water (water used after making spaghetti) and whatever leftovers we had, as well as the old stuff from the A & P. The pigs loved all of it and they grew quite large.

My pig was named Blacky—a very large pig, you could hardly see his legs because he was so fat and his skin was mostly black with a little white. As he was my favorite, I tried to ride him every so often. Sometimes I got as far as thirty or forty yards.

When it was killing time, Grandma did everything. She had one of us take the pig to the old apple tree that we had on our property and tie his hind legs to the rope that was attached to a top branch. There was a block and tackle and we winched the poor pig up high enough so that Grandma was at the proper height to stab it in the neck. She made sure that Grandpa was next to her with a large bucket to catch the blood that shot out of the animal.

This was a painful thing for me. I was so fond of all the pigs. Listening to their cries was extremely difficult, but there was nothing I could do about it.

Once the pig was dead, Grandpa left with his bucket of hot blood. This was used to make blood pudding. They made it into a pie shape and they would eat it in slices. I could not even try it. Anyway, Grandma got scalding water and soaked the pig with a rag as it hung there. Then she shaved the very coarse hair off it.

I did not stay around for the cutting up of the pig and how they knew exactly what part was to be hung in our cellar with plenty of salt wrapped around the meat to cure as they have done for years and years.

A great deal of the meat was put aside to make sausage. We had a hand crank device and you put the pig meat in it along with some special spices that Grandma had. Then we filled casings from a local Italian store with the ground pork and spices.

Although most of it was air dried, a lot was cooked for the special Sunday meal.

The dried sausage was stored (once Grandpa would give the word that it was cured) in large Mason jars that were filled with lard. In this way you could keep the sausage fresh forever. When you wanted some sausage, you opened up the jar, wiped away the lard, and ate it as it was. Of course, you could also cook it.

So as you can see I had plenty of work at home. Plus school work and athletic activities. The driving force of my life, however, was making money. My mother had to give Grandpa a carton of Camels each week just for taking her to work

I had to pay Grandma thirty-five dollars a week for room and board. Let me tell you, that was a lot of money for a twelve-year-old, but Mother knew that I made fifty to sixty dollars each week working at my various enterprises.

I agreed to my payment schedule. And that agreement stayed till the day I walked away from 316 Garfield Street. I guess I was lucky—they never raised my fee for staying there.

You may ask why I have not mentioned Aldo throughout this entire episode. What were his duties and obligations? For some reason the first born boy in Italy is something special. He, by way of this birthright, could be helpful or not, as far as the household expenses and work were concerned. Aldo chose to contribute nothing.

My mother's excuse for him was that he was not as agile or as talented as I was at doing things. I was less likely to get hurt, she said. When it came to the financial assistance of the family, I was the one who spoke the best English, and who made the most money. Therefore I was the chosen one; the one chosen to labor for the general good of everyone else. I stopped trying to figure that out when I was an adult. However, when my mother passed away on her ninety-first birthday, nothing had changed. I was still the one who was responsible for everyone.

Chapter Eleven

Chuck was a big guy who always had a cigar in his mouth. He owned the Berkeley Heights hardware store and one day I just asked him for some work—any work. I was thirteen at the time, and Chuck knew who I was. He saw my picture in the paper when I was praised for a soccer victory and he also saw me ice skating on the pond across from the police station.

So Chuck decided to try me out and he gave me odd jobs at the hardware store.

"How much do want an hour?" he asked.

"I'd rather work for items that you sell in the store."

He nodded. "That's OK."

For me it was a good deal. I could get equipment for the things I sold—bike parts and such. Chuck got me, a really good worker, for no wages, just for the wholesale cost of his goods. It worked out for both of us.

For a while I worked to earn a toaster for Grandpa. He did not have one, but once I brought it home to him, he ate toast and jelly every day.

Chuck liked me a lot and I liked him as well. I am sure he has no idea how much he affected me in a positive way. I continued to work for things that I needed and that were useful to my sideline business. I worked for a sled, and a baseball glove, a bat, fishing pole, and for the things I fixed up and sold. Chuck and I became such good friends that he and his wife trusted me to watch their two little girls. I did jobs at his house too, gardening, concrete work and painting.

I did not realize that a few townspeople saw me running around and going from this job to that, and calling me "the Little Whore." Someone would see me dangling from some rooftop in Summit painting the eaves. Someone else would see me cutting the grass at a house in New Providence. Or I might be waxing a car in Gillette.

I always thumbed a ride and I always got one. In the car I told the driver where I was going and what I was doing, and the next thing was that they asked if I would work for them, and I did.

One of my main goals at this time was to get my own brand new bicycle.

I was promised a bike back in Italy from my mother. She said, "If you keep out of trouble and pass into the third grade, I'll buy you a bike so you won't need to rent one."

Well, I passed that test with flying colors, and I said to my mother, "Can I have my bike now?"

My mother sighed. "One of your sisters stole the money I saved for your bike, Franco. Next year, OK?"

I said, "All right."

And the next year, when I passed again, I asked for my bike again.

"Oh, you don't need a bike now, we're going to America."

So it goes and there it went—nowhere for me.

But there was a Sears store in Summit NJ. I went there and I could not believe all the beautiful bikes of various kinds. I wanted one with big fat tires and foot brakes and streamers on the handlebar grips. The bike cost twenty-eight dollars. I had it and I bought it for cash. What a great feeling I had riding it home. That five miles went by in a flash.

Now I was sort of a free man. I could control my schedule as I needed to—I had wheels!

School was going well and home was, well, a place to sleep. Aldo and I shared a room upstairs and there was a single bathroom downstairs. There was large kitchen and two bedrooms on the first floor. One was Grandpa and Suzy's and the other was my mother's.

In the summertime we sweated and stuck to the sheets at night. But in the winter we got as close as possible to the radiators and still the upstairs was pretty cold. Aldo and I spent many nights down in the cellar in the summer even though I must admit I was quite scared, especially after watching some horror show like *The Mummy's Hand* with Boris Karloff or *The Werewolf of London* with Lon Chaney.

Grandma Suzy had very strict rules with regard to my conduct, but also my mother's and Aldo's. She used to say to me, "You better do as I say or I will send you to the Boys' Home." I did not know exactly what the Boys' Home was but I imagined it was a kind of prison for teenagers. No one was allowed to open the refrigerator more than once a night. "You had better know what you are looking for because the cold will come out and it costs a lot of money to replace it."

We were not allowed to take showers or baths too often, as it was very costly to heat the water. I showered as much as possible at gym class and only used the shower at home for special occasions. You could only turn the TV knob clockwise, very slowly. If you did pass a channel you wanted to watch (when Grandma was not watching *The Secret Storm* or *The Edge Of Night* or *Arthur Godfrey*) you had to continue going around again to get to your channel. If you turned backwards she would throw a fit. The couch with the heavy plastic cover was off-limits for me but it would be OK for a guest to sit on. I was not allowed to use the front door. Grandma Suzy said, "The front door is for company—not you."

No doubt, Grandma had a mean streak and I could never understand why she was so hard on me. I did most of the chores that needed to be done as well as pay thirty-five dollars every week, never complaining about it. I knew none of my friends paid anything to live at home, but I just accepted that I had a different life. I realized that I was living with grandparents and their rules, or rather Suzy's were harsh. Sometimes I had to go into my savings to meet my weekly obligation. Actually I did it more for my mother than anyone else.

There were also some severe restrictions on food. During the workweek, we ate poorly. Dandelion (picked from the yard) and vinegar and polenta were not an uncommon meal. However, when

Sunday came around all of Grandma Suzy's friends appeared for dinner, which was served at one o'clock in the afternoon.

We had Arlene and her fireman husband from East Orange, Frank and Kekie and their daughter who was a little slow from Newark, Uncle Joe whom we called Foxie. He was a bricklayer and the brother of my grandfather's second wife. He was a nice man and he was there every Sunday; sometimes he only took a cup of coffee.

Grandma served many kinds of macaroni and Italian red sauce with *braciole*. These were thin steaks rolled up with spices inside and held together either by toothpicks or thread. There were beef bones, home made sausage, hot and mild, and of course meatballs. She also had chicken, fried or cacciatore. We often played cards for pennies but we had to make sure that at the end of the day Grandpa won or there would be some big fights.

On the table there were quart size bottles of Rheingold Beer and for the Americans, Four Roses whiskey. After dinner we always had *finocchio*. This is fennel which looks like celery and smells like licorice. Then there were chestnuts and Grandpa would always sip a little strong Italian liquor called Strega or another type of strong liquor called Fernet.

Another duty of mine was to deliver meals that Grandma cooked for certain people. I delivered these specialty items to as many as six or seven homes. On a bike, one at a time, this was not easy. This was a grand gesture on her part, but I knew that at least some of it was covered by my contributions.

Naturally, the company that used the front door on Sunday left with more than they brought. They stocked up on every kind of morsel imaginable and they staggered out the door with them.

Once that big meal was past, we were back to the strictest rules. To this day I can not understand it. When the company left, Suzy's smile did, too. Then, for the rest of the week she was a cross between a warden and a witch.

Chapter Twelve

I graduated from eighth grade and left Columbia school and the next big step was high school. The town of Berkeley Heights did not have a high school although they were building one very close to the now famous Bell Laboratories that launched the first "Telstar" satellite. Anyway, the School would be called Governor Livingston Regional High, but for now, in 1959, we were forced to travel fifteen miles to Jonathon Dayton in Springfield, New Jersey.

I had been the big guy in our little school. Now I was thrown into a regional system that included much tougher areas than the rural Italian town of Berkeley Heights, which we sometimes referred to as Little Italy.

I vowed that I would stand my ground and not be intimidated by anyone. As it turned out, on the second day of school as a freshman, a big guy named Walter went straight for me. We were walking in the hallway between classes, and Walter would not move out of my way. Well, he was the big shot, the leader of a gang.

I stared at Walter. Then I said, "If you're looking for someone to push around, you got the wrong guy."

He had a bulldog's head and the body of a fat heavyweight wrestler.

Walter tried to grin me down. But he was a little shorter than I was and I bore into him with my own unwavering stare.

He said nothing, but I noticed his fists were clenched.

"Go ahead," I offered, "take your best shot."

Walter withered under my glare. He hesitated, then moved sheepishly back to his buddies who all had open mouths.

It is strange how the word gets around. The next thing I knew there were juniors as well as seniors who wanted to meet this Franco, and see what was up.

I met with one of these seniors at the track in gym class. We had to do the mandatory quarter mile run before any other activity. When this guy saw the shape I was in, he was friendly to me and he introduced me to his friends, too. As a gesture—and to prove to them that I was more than their equal—I asked one of them to punch me as hard as he could in my stomach or chest area. One fellow came up and he was shy about letting me have it, but finally hit me with a haphazard blow. I laughed. "Hey," I told him, "hit me square, you won't hurt me."

So he reeled back and hit me for all he was worth. His blow caused me to step back some from the force, but it did not bother me at all. The guy was impressed and he asked, "How did you get in that kind of condition?"

I told him, "Well, I have worked all my life and I do not go out of my way to lift or anything. I just work long hours and hard, but I hit a lot harder than I take."

From that moment on, I was the big guy and actually I was not a bully but I did not want to go around the school looking behind my back.

It was difficult playing sports now that the school was so far from my home. If I stayed late for team practice, I could not work the jobs to pay Suzy. Nor could I buy the clothes I wore. I was still employed by Chuck at the hardware store and at his home and also at the local Gulf Station. At the station I pumped gas, and on my own time, I learned how to work on car engines. I also met a lot of nice people.

So for a while my routine was school till five, go home, change, eat something quick, and run to the station. I was home by eleven and hard at my books until after midnight.

On weekends it was a combination of Gulf, Chuck's Hardware and any other job I could line up. Finally, the following year when I was a sophomore, Governor Livingston High was completed on top of a big hill in Berkeley Heights.

I was treated like a senior because I had a great reputation as an athlete.

I did everything equally well—football, soccer, baseball and basketball. The most influential person in my life at this time was Coach Hunchar. He was head of the athletic department. Hunchar was a rugged looking ex-Marine, who was in great shape, and he exacted discipline over his students. He liked me from the start, possibly because I was so competitive. Or maybe it was because I cracked his ribs the first time we met. We were at gym class and in front of all the kids. Hunchar read from his roster list and called out everyone's name, and made a few crisp comments to let us know that he knew us.

When he got to my name, he said, "Hey, Franco I hear that you think you're pretty strong."

"No more than the next guy," I said.

"Why don't you come down from the bleachers and show me."

Obediently, I stepped down from where I was sitting and faced Coach Hunchar. He was built like a boxer, and in fact I had heard he was Golden Gloves champion in the Marines.

"Why don't you give me a good hard squeeze and show me how strong you are, Franco?" Coach Hunchar had very blue eyes that twinkled when he spoke. His eyebrows were bushy and he had very straight teeth.

"I couldn't do that, Coach."

"Why not?"

"I don't want to get into trouble for hurting a teacher."

"That's all right, Franco. Try it."

So, I squeezed him around the ribs, and I heard a gasp, and then I let go of him.

Coach Hunchar said, "Well, I guess you are pretty strong."

He had us do some laps then, and after this, he dismissed the class and went to his office. The next day I heard that I had cracked two of his ribs. But that did not stop our friendship. It made it. I can not tell you how close we became. In many ways he was like a father to me. At one point, when I had had enough pressure from Suzy, and I couldn't take it anymore, I told Coach I was going to quit school so I could work full time.

Well, he sat me down in his office, and he cracked my ribs—with words.

He said, "Franco, that is very short-sighted. I thought you could see far into the future. Do you want to blow your chances for a good career? What about all of your talent? Are you going to waste it? What you have going for you is God-given. Most kids would give anything to have your abilities and you are about to throw them away."

Then he held up his little finger, and he was so angry I thought he was going to stick me in the eye with it. "You see this, Franco?"

I said, "Yes."

"Well, you have more talent in your pinkie than most kids have in their whole body. And your mind, well, it works faster than a boxer's fists. Don't tell me you're going to quit high school because I don't want to hear it."

Coach Hunchar's blue eyes were not twinkling; they were burning ice.

I nodded, shrugged. "I guess you're right, Coach."

"Darn right I'm right, now get out of here before I have to crack your ribs."

We both laughed.

I started to give him a hug. He quickly stepped backward, narrowed his eyes.

"Get outta here," he joked.

I did, and I did not think of quitting school again.

Chapter Thirteen

Coach Hunchar was right. I did well in school because it came naturally to me. But I spent more time calculating ways to make money than I did on homework. There was no choice; I had to. At home we still had our Sunday dinners and I managed to do my jobs for Grandma, plus the delivery service. But as soon as I was able to get away from the house, I went to the Gulf station or anywhere else where I could make a buck.

Junior year I got my drivers license—and a car. A 1947 Plymouth. I paid forty dollars for it and my cousin Joey and I painted it bright blue with a four-inch brush.

From far away it looked pretty good but up close you could see every brush stroke.

No matter, the car was just to fool around in the back yard behind Grandpa's garden. I burned rubber in the dirt and got the feel of a speed shifter on the column.

We had a ball with that car and I can remember sleeping in it many nights in the back of the house. I slept in it not so much because I wanted to, but because Suzy had her rules. I was not allowed to stay out after ten in the evening. If I came home after ten the doors would be locked and I would have to find a place to sleep. I used to sleep in Grandpa's car till I got mine. The bad thing about sleeping outside was that in the summer it was hot. If you cracked the window, the mosquitoes ate you alive.

Many mornings I went into the house covered with dried blood.

One Friday night there was a teen dance at one of the schools. I had learned to do the box step, and I enjoyed going to these teen nights, as they called them. But since the dances were over at ten and I lived four miles from home, I always had to race back a few minutes before the hour to beat Suzy's curfew. Sometimes I made it with only a few seconds to spare. Grandma was always right there, ready to lock me out. One time when I was dancing with my girlfriend, Shirley, I looked at my watch and it was five to ten. So I apologized to her and raced home. I beat all my previous records, but when I approached the back door at a run, I was knocked down by a huge blow to my forehead.

The noise was loud enough to disturb my mother, who was watching TV. She came out to see what it was. I was lying on my back with a huge knot on my head from hitting the porch that Grandpa had built that day. The overhead shed roof was five foot eight.

I was almost six-foot at the time.

I spoke to Grandpa when he came out to see what was going on. "How come you built it so low?" I asked, rubbing my head.

He got underneath the roof and raised his hand over his head.

"Plenty of room," he said.

"But, Grandpa, you know I've been breaking light bulbs with my head lately. Didn't you know I was going to have a hard time with this?"

He shrugged, and said, "Pay attention next time."

Either he did not want me growing any taller or he wanted to take me down a few inches—either way, my head hurt.

I had a similar thing happen one night. Suzy had Grandpa put up a new clothesline while I was away at work. Once again I was trying to beat curfew and this time I ran into a thick rope at eye level. It spun me violently to the ground and I had a painful rope burn that took weeks to go away. It was easier dealing with the pain than explaining the injury to my friends at school. Mostly I did not tell them anything. They had no idea of the life I lived on Garfield Street.

My next real road car was a 1949 Ford with a flathead eight cylinder engine.

It was in a little rough shape so I paid eighty dollars for it and started to fix it up at the Gulf station. I sanded it down to bare metal, took off all the chrome, and had it decked and rolled. Then I opened up the back fenders like a Buick. I got a few cans of light gray primer (primer is very forgiving and does not show runs) and primed the whole car.

I thought it was really cool.

At the same time I was doing well at school and my sports activities were going smoothly. The teams I was on even got some county and state awards. All of this achievement meant nothing to my family. They told me it was a big waste of time and I should come to work at McGregors.

My next automobile was called Mr. Horsepower. This one was a 1953 Mercury with a huge Oldsmobile engine that had 3 deuces for carbs, a 4/11 posi rear and a La Salle transmission, all of which translated to speed from the word go. The hood had over 100 louvers and it was a beautiful blue color, not painted with a brush.

Mr. Horsepower looked cool and so did I with a cigarette dangling on my lip for effect.

However, now my expenses became demanding and I had less time to work, so things were quite difficult for me. I was dating my girlfriend Shirley full time. I never felt like cheating on her, not once. If you are going to have a relationship with somebody, you better be honest about it, and I was.

So now I had a steady girl and life was pretty good. The only problem was that I was short on cash. The food and lodging bill came due every week. Thirty-five dollars, rain or shine. As usual I was always hustling to make money.

There was this homely sort of fellow named Curt who always wanted to be part of the gang, but never made it somehow. I suggested to him one day that he should join a sport and make friends that way. "I'm no good at sports," he replied. I could see why, he was overweight, never exercised and he walked as if he were carrying a sack of potatoes.

"Why don't you try out for water boy on the soccer team?" I offered.

"You think you could get me in?"

I spoke to Coach Hunchar, and Curtis had a job.

You never saw anyone as proud and diligent as Curtis and I think he lost some weight running around, too. Plus he made friends with everyone on the team.

Anyway, one day he heard me talking about how I was always short of cash, and he said he could help me there.

"How?" I asked.

"Well," he said, "I have access to certain products that you might sell at a profit."

"What kinds of products?" I asked.

"Almost anything you want," he said confidently.

I looked suspiciously at him.

"What will I have to pay?"

"Nothing," said Curt with a smile.

At first I thought he was joking.

But the next day he brought me a brand new Panasonic portable radio.

This was a popular item that retailed for thirty dollars. I told Curt I thought I could sell the radio in town, and I did, for fifteen dollars. When I told him about it, he smiled. The next day Curt came to school with a half dozen brand new Panasonic radios, and he gave every one of them to me and would not take a penny from me when I sold them all in—believe it or not—under thirty minutes.

I began getting orders for unusual items. A bunch of teachers requested Kaywoodie pipes. I had never heard of them, but Curt had. A day after I mentioned the pipes Curt brought a bag of them to the Gulf station. I looked in the bag and there were twenty pipes worth thirty a piece in there. Again I sold the pipes for half price and I got rid of them in no time flat. My financial problem was going away. But, you know, I had never asked Curt exactly where he was getting these things. I found out from his brother that he was simply buying them and giving them to me. That same day I found out how rich he was and how he felt about me. He had never had any friends in his life, and now, thanks to his work on the soccer team, he had more buddies than he could count.

Everybody liked Curt.

Especially me.

Chapter Fourteen

After the big pipe sale, however, I decided I could not take advantage of Curt's generosity. I told him he did not have to give me anything to be his friend because I was his friend. He hung his head and said, "If you ever need anything . . . I mean anything."

I was on the prowl for regular jobs that I could do before or after the Gulf station work. So I went to nearby Summit and there was an expensive hotel there called The Suburban. I applied for a job as a bellhop. I told them I could only work there on weekends in the very early hours, and they hired me.

My first day on the job I learned that the workers from the Ciba chemical company stayed there. They tipped miserably. The unwritten rule was that you should tip at least twenty-five cents per bag. These so called professionals tipped twenty-five cents for four bags. However, I noticed the old ladies that lived in the hotel full time and many of them seemed lonely. So I walked them to the front door when they went to church and did the same when they came back.

At first they tried to tip me a quarter and I would not take it. Eventually, though, they forced dollar bills on me. They rolled them up really thin and squeezed them into my palm. Now I was making a few good dollars at my bellhop job and at my informal escort service.

One weekend morning I walked by the kitchen of the hotel. The cook saw me. He was a large black man and he called me over and said, "You new here?"

"Pretty new."

"Had breakfast yet?"

I shook my head.

"Want something?"

"I don't think I'm allowed to have breakfast on the job."

"Nonsense," he replied. "Well, I don't have any money."

He said, "How do you like your omelets?"

I told him that I liked anything any way it was prepared.

So he made me a beautiful Denver omelet, the first one I ever had.

He also placed two link sausages next to it and two pieces of toast and two tabs of marmalade. I had never seen marmalade either. I enjoyed every morsel I put in my mouth.

I think my friend the cook got a great deal of pleasure watching me eat his meal.

Whenever he was on duty, he repeated that same kindness. I thought it was truly amazing how people read other people, how they know one another so quickly. He knew, for instance, that I could never ask for food. He also knew that I was hungry much of the time. His kindness was like a beacon in the darkness. He and Curt and Coach Hunchar and Chuck and all the others were my saviors along the rocky road of my young life.

My senior year in high school was hard for me. My friends were focused on getting into college. I knew I could do that, too. But at night all I heard was that I did not spend enough time at home. I was told that I should be paying fifty dollars a week instead of thirty-five. Actually, I contributed a lot more when you added up all the extras.

"What if I want to go to college?" I said one night.

Grandma Suzy gasped. "If you do, we will all die!" she exclaimed.

"How is that?" I asked.

"There would not be enough money coming in," my mother added.

I told them I would not leave them high and dry. I could work at college, too. Still, the pressure they put on me got me all confused. Even if it was not true, I felt I was abandoning them when they needed me. Maybe college was not in the cards.

However, Coach Hunchar said it was. He had worked with a number of colleges and he was sure he could get me a scholarship. I kept this in mind, but my responsibilities prevented me from doing anything about it.

I had all I could do to meet the rising cost of living at home. More often than not I was asked for fifty a week rather than thirty-five. I kept my car, my girlfriend, my sports, my jobs and my schoolwork intact. It was a juggling act, but somehow I managed to do it successfully.

Graduation came sooner than I would have liked. The most difficult part about it came after the ceremony. The parents were so proud of their children. There was a lot of hugging and kissing and back patting going around. I looked around and in that sea of faces, I saw no one from my household—not even my brother. I felt ashamed.

My family thought so little of this event, they did not bother to attend. I had to sneak away, so no one would see that I was such a lonely individual.

To tell the truth, some very scary things went through my mind at that time. And I thank God I overcame those foolish ideas.

Chapter Fifteen

All during my senior year Grandma Suzy had a rule about no girls were to come to the house. This became ironclad after Aldo got his girlfriend pregnant. They were married behind the altar of The Little Flower Catholic Church, and then things were better for them, but not for me.

They threw me out of the room I shared with Aldo and after that I lived in a makeshift storage room unless I came in late. Then, as always, I slept in my car.

Aldo's son was born healthy and his name, of course, was Joseph, but everyone called him Joey right from the start. My mother and grandmother pretty much raised Joey. But—getting back to my situation—I was not permitted to have any girlfriends in, or near, the house.

That made it hard on Shirley, who was with me almost all of the time I was not at home. Once she came over however, and she was actually allowed to enter through the front door. On the other side of the threshold was Grandma, who gave Shirley the third degree. She grilled her like a police officer.

"Why are you here?"

Shirley said, "I brought Franco some things he needs for a school project."

"Sit there on the couch."

When I came downstairs I saw Shirley sitting on the edge of the couch that I was not allowed to sit on. She looked ill at ease, so I quickly introduced her to everyone. That did not really help, as no one said anything after that.

Then Shirley whispered to me that she had to go to the bathroom.

Grandma followed her right up to the door and stood guard outside of the tiny door as if to let me know that I was not coming anywhere near her.

All at once, Shirley screamed.

The bathroom door flew open and almost knocked Grandma to the floor. This was hard to do, as her big feet were always planted like cinderblocks.

The first thought that went through my mind was that Grandma had done something mean to Shirley. But the way she explained it, when she went to sit down on the toilet she heard a sloshing sound in the tub. Surprised, she drew the plastic curtain aside.

Her face was white when she exclaimed, "There's a bunch of snakes in the bathtub."

My mother and Grandma started to laugh.

I poked my head in the bathroom and saw the eels that Grandpa had brought back from his shopping trip in Newark. Grandma kept the eels alive until she was ready to kill them later that day prior to making eels in red sauce.

You can just imagine how embarrassed I was, with Shirley scared half-to-death, and my mother and Grandma cackling over this humorous event, and me wanting to be anywhere but in my own home.

Believe it or not, this little crisis made my mother and Suzy like Shirley. So she was allowed to visit me after that, but under extremely close scrutiny.

Sometimes I wondered what Shirley would think if she ate dinner at our house. My mother loved to cook squirrels. To me they tasted like rubber bands. The only thing that made them all right to eat was the Italian red sauce that was so delicious you could pour it on rocks and they would have tasted good.

We did eat some odd food, though. Thank God no one came to our dinner table to witness, or worse, eat, these unusual dishes.

We had a split baby calf's head. The head was placed in a large pan with one eye looking to the left and the other split head eye to the right. The heads would be surrounded by sliced potatoes that were baked with the head till golden. At the table it was a ritual that Grandpa would get the brains and Grandma would always get at least one of the eyes and part of the tongue and everyone else would fight for the cheek and gums.

Not very pretty but actually tasted all right at the time.

One night we had chicken cacciatore. The chickens were very tiny, indeed.

"What kind of chickens are these?" I asked.

"Spring chickens," Grandpa answered.

I ate twenty before I was full.

Afterwards I went out to the porch where Grandpa was smoking a Camel. Something seemed different. It was very quiet out there. I looked around. I did not see our homing pigeons, which were usually cooing and flying around the porch.

"Where are my birds?" I asked Grandpa.

"You ate 'em," he replied. He burst out laughing.

One of my many chores was taking care of our real chickens. I used to invent little games to break up the boredom of doing tasks. For instance, I decided to put a string on the chicken coop door, so that I could catch chickadees that flew inside to get the grain. At a moment's notice I could yank the door closed and catch a wild bird.

Well, some days I caught a lot of them. I would go into the coop and they were all flying around, and I would catch some and hold them, and eventually let them go.

Once I put a whole bunch of the little birds into my shirt. They fluttered around not actually hurting but tickling me. I would release them two at a time, one in each hand, watching them explode away into the sunlight.

My mother saw me do this, and she called from the porch, "What are you doing?"

"Nothing," I told her.

She came down to the field in front of the chicken coup and discovered my little game with the chickadees. Without a word, she smacked me on the back of my head with her powerful right hand.

She said with a scowl, "We can eat those!"

"What are you talking about? These are chickadees!" I protested.

Now, this was in Italian because the only English words my mother had learned in the past eight years were "shurrup"(shutup) and "sonofabitch".

After that, I had to keep my mother stocked up with chickadees for her miniature bird cacciatore dinners.

Chapter Sixteen

I was out of school for one week when I heard that American Motors was opening a new facility in Mountainside, New Jersey. A neighbor of mine, Mr. Bellamy, told me about the possibility of a job. He was a comptroller for AMC and he said the new warehouse was going to need installation workers the following Saturday.

A lot of people tried out for the job, which was to set up the warehouse as fast as possible. One, in particular, was a fortyish fellow named George. He had no fingers on his left hand, just his thumb. It was amazing how he could smoke a cigarette by holding it between his thumb and his palm. None of us knew how large the crew was that would be hired once the facility was complete, but the whole bunch of us that morning were hired at minimum wage to set things up. The big boss that ran the warehouse was Mr. Anthony DiBona and his assistant was Michael Miele.

I figured if I worked hard and kept my nose clean, I had as good a chance as anyone to get hired full time. Actually, I ran circles around most of the workers that day. I think I was the only one who had a positive attitude. Another blessing is that I was always a "morning person." I could go to bed at two AM and still hop out of bed at six with a smile on my face.

So the days passed and I was always on time and I worked harder than anyone except maybe George did. One morning Mr. Miele took me to the side and asked, "How are all these new guys working out?" I wondered whether he had asked them the same question.

"I don't really watch how others do their job because I am so busy doing mine," I told him. "But there's one guy you got to admire, and that's George over there."

Mr. Miele was surprised that I mentioned George. "I saw that he had a hard time hanging from the uprights when we were putting them together," he said.

"That's true," I said, "but when we are done with the warehouse, how often are we going to hang from the uprights?"

Mr. Miele replied, "Never."

I said, "George is dependable, and because of his disability, I know for sure that he's a team player. As for the rest, I can't really say."

He looked briefly into my eyes, and nodded.

I am not sure what that did or did not do for either of us that day, but George and I became employees of American Motors in July of 1963.

So now I was a full time employee starting at eighty-two dollars a week and earning four thousand dollars a year. That was a lot of money for someone just out of high school and I went to see my neighbor, Mr. Bellamy, to thank him, but he said he had nothing to do with it. That made me feel even better, as I had proved myself without any help. The actual competition in the real world had begun, and I had won the first round.

I did not stop working at the Gulf station, though. I found another job as a part-time shoe salesperson at the Blue Star Shopping Center earning $1.10 per hour plus commission.

Then I met this pretty girl named Bette Ann Korker, who lived near the Center.

At this time I was driving a black 1957 Buick Special Convertible. I had purchased it a few months earlier from a doctor at the Summit Hospital and it was a beautiful car in perfect condition. It had six speakers and all that chrome, and I looked good coming and going.

Anyway, I met Bette Ann and her mother Mary, and I managed to politely get her phone number. They lived in Fanwood, which was about eight miles from my home.

One day just before starting the shoe sales job I drove by Bette Ann's house. I did that a few times, but I saw no one out in the yard. Finally, I got up the nerve to call her and I asked her out on a date. "We're having a picnic at the house on Saturday and you're welcome to come over," she said.

"I'll be there," I told her.

Now I was in an emotional bind. I did not believe in being unfaithful and here I was going out with Shirley (had been for a year or more) and now . . . what was I doing? Cheating was not frowned upon by either my mother or my brother, and in fact they thought it was human nature to do so. But to me it was all wrong. I was close friends with Shirley's sister Barbara and her mother, too. What was I to do?

In the meantime, I eased my mind by finding another job, this time at the local ice skating rink. There was a skating contest and I won it, and the prize was a trophy and a job. So now I had more part time jobs than I had time to do them, but still I worked them all in somehow. The ice rink was a nighttime thing, a skating guard, but when the boss heard that I was a swimmer, too, he gave me a swimming test for the pool next door. I passed his test with flying colors and now I was also a part time lifeguard. After hours, which meant late at night, I drove the old Willys Jeep that had a squeegee that smoothed the ice on the rink, and so you could add that to my growing list of employment opportunities. Skate hard, six to eight. After that I would clean the ice until ten. On certain days I alternated with the other lifeguard from eight to ten. So I was into water and ice and shoes and automobile parts and gasoline pumps.

Somehow I managed to get to bed by midnight.

At last I spoke with Shirley about my upcoming picnic with Bette Ann and her family. I did not play it down nor did I play it up. I just stated facts.

Well, as I had figured, Shirley blew up. We were in my Buick at the time, and when she finished screaming at me, she got out and ripped the antenna right out off the fender and stomped off.

I think that that was the last time I saw her.

Chapter Seventeen

I told my mother that Shirley and I had a little fight, as no doubt, they had watched it from a window of the house. I wanted to set the record straight.

Surprising to me was how upset they were. Shirley was not Italian, but they really liked her. In their mind I had to marry her because she had stepped into our home, she was respectable and well mannered—and how could I dare not marry her? They also knew how serious she was about me.

"How would you feel if she killed herself?" my mother asked me.

"I will decide who I marry and who I don't...."

Mother and Grandma cast hateful glances at me.

"Besides, I want to see another girl," I told them.

Was I ever the bastard then. Their faces boiled with scorn.

However, I went to Bette Ann's picnic the following day.

First, I stopped by the bakery and bought a popular beehive cake (it had nuts, caramel and lots of whipped cream, and it was cold) and I also got cannoli (Italian pastry) and a few eclairs and Napoleons.

This set me back a pretty penny, but the first impression is critical, as I had learned in everything I had ever done. I arrived at Bette Ann's with my radio much louder than it should have been. Of course the top was down; it was always down unless it was raining or thirty below. I parked swiftly and assuredly between some closely placed cars. I did this in one quick shot so they knew that I could also drive.

To my surprise, Bette Ann was just as excited as I was. She ran out to meet me and could not wait to introduce me to her family and friends. I had already met her mother Mary, now I met her older brother, who was known as Freddy or little Fred although he was six feet four inches tall. Bette Ann's dad, Fred

Sr. was a slender six-one. I soon discovered that he came from a German background while Mary was Scotch-Irish, as they say. Bette Ann's sister, whose name was Betty, lived a few houses down from them. Her husband Tony Farinola, Uncle Tony, they called him, was Italian.

Fred seemed to know various things about me. I guess he had heard them from Bette Ann. He was asking me questions that only someone with prior knowledge would ask.

"You seem to be in tiptop shape," he said.

"I'm okay."

Believe it or not, Fred did the exact same thing that Coach Hunchar did four years earlier. He asked me to prove my strength by giving him a big bear hug.

"I don't think so."

"Why not?"

"What is it about grown ups and their bear hugs?"

"Seriously," he said. "Give me a squeeze so I can see how strong you really are."

"I don't think I should do that."

"Afraid I can't take it?"

So I told him about Coach Hunchar, and what happened. Fred just laughed.

So with him bracing himself, I gave him the same little squeeze I gave the coach.

Surprised, Fred glanced at Mary, and said, in a faint voice, "This guinea is powerful."

I took the remark in my stride, as I knew he did not mean it the way it sounded.

Anyway, what in the hell could I do about it?

I can honestly say that in a very short time, Fred accepted me as a son.

Then, for the first time, I had a real family. I felt sorry for my breakup with Shirley. But, in a way, this had to happen. Shirley came from a broken home just like I did.

The atmosphere in the Korker family was beyond a dream.

My life was working out beautifully.

I went to work every day at American Motors. Then to the shoe store. After that, the Gulf Station. Then, if I was not on duty at the rink or the pool, I headed to Howard Johnson on route 22 in North Plainfield, and I got a hand-packed quart of ice cream and brought it to Bette Ann's in Fanwood. Mary made tea and Ovaltine and sometimes matzohs with butter.

By this time I was promoted from a parts picker to an order interpreter. This means I took orders from dealers over the telephone. Their needs were then put onto IBM cards, and orders were generated from them. I was making over five thousand a year. This was the big time for a kid just out of school. Now I wanted to buy my first new car. I still faithfully paid thirty-five dollars every week to Grandma Suzy for food, which I rarely ate and lodging which was not much better than a storage room.

As it turned out my friend Jimmy LaSasso was also in a market for a new car so we both went out and bought two brand new 1964 XL convertible Fords.

My Ford was all blue with a blue interior and it was powered with a 352 V/8 complete with bucket seats and an automatic shift on the floor. Jimmy bought a red convertible with a 390 V/8 and a white interior.

My new car listed for $4,122.00. The payments were $99.33 a month for four years. I was now the King of the Hop. I had the car, the girl, the job, the family and everything I had ever wanted. I was nineteen years old, but somehow I knew I would soon want more.

Chapter Eighteen

T he selling of shoes was an art in which I got very good, very quickly.

The store was set up to take care of women at one end, men at an other, and there was a "pit", as we called it, for kids. All the salesmen took a turn in working the pit because there you sold the least and had the largest returns.

The men were the easiest sell. They usually knew what they wanted and they also knew their shoe size. You could advise them of a special deal, purchasing a second pair or possibly an accessory item and they would go for it. The kids were more difficult. You measured the foot and advised the parent what was the best thing to do in terms of growing into the shoe. You talked about wearability and style, blisters when the shoe was too loose or too tight. But you could only go so far with good advice. Mothers insisted that they knew what they were doing when they bought the incorrect size for their son or daughter. And the day the shoes were returned, you were always off duty and the manager always gave them a refund, and you lost the sale. Still, the manager kept to the store policy, which was to make sure the customer was happy.

Sales of girls' and women's shoes were extremely difficult in one way and very easy in another. There was the young lady who came in with mom who would have a long list of shoes to bring out, usually thirty minutes before closing time. We knew this type quite well. I went behind the wall where the inventory was stored. After a few minutes I reappeared, saying, "I'm so sorry, the ones you want aren't in stock right now. However, here are some that would look just as well on you."

We also went out of our way to bring out styles on a special promotion that gave the salesperson two to three times the normal commission.

If the customer said, "I did not request that shoe!" I came back with—"But it will look so good on your foot . . . your height is just right for this . . . your legs will be accentuated with this style." If the customer still was not sure, and asked another salesperson for advice, he always said, "That's perfect on you—but I thought we sold out. That style flew off the shelf it was so popular!"

Needless to say, we all did well working together like this.

The biggest problem was the pushy person who bought an expensive shoe for a specific occasion and then returned it the next day. Naturally, the salesperson always got the blame. We also sold shoes and purses that were specially dyed just for the customer. There were signs all over the store that stated these items could not be returned, but some people demanded refunds—for reasons beyond anyone's imagination—and some of these people got away with it because their complaints wore down our manager.

Every so often a beautiful woman would come in and we knew how to take her shoe off and hold her leg in such a way that the salespeople behind the shoe wall could see up her dress. We were shocked a number of times at women who did not wear any undergarments. We thought that was cool at the time, but now I think quite differently about it. But I guess compared to the things that go on today it was not that bad.

While my adventures in the shoe trade continued, my relationship with Bette Ann and the family was so wonderful that they began including me in all the things they did together. One night Fred said to me "You want to go to dinner with us on Friday?"

I glanced at Bette Ann, who was smiling, and I said, "Sure, Fred."

We met at their house as planned. A mile down the road next to Route 22 was a popular family restaurant called Snuffy's Tavern. It was known mostly for its steaks but also for the long bar and the stuffed toy monkey on a long wire that was used to take orders from the bar to the kitchen.

A waiter would attach an order to the monkey and with a quick push, the monkey went flying down the wire to the kitchen window. Once the cook retrieved the order he would slide the monkey back out for additional order taking. Children—and adults, too—always had their eyes trained on that monkey.

Well, that night, we all sat down at this big round table and there were five in our party. Mary, whom I called Mom, (and still do to this day) Fred, Freddy, Bette Ann and me. They ordered Rob Roys and Bette Ann and I had iced tea. Then everyone began staring at the menu.

Now, I have to confess that I was eighteen years old and I had never been in a restaurant before. To tell the truth, I was scared. I felt that everyone was watching me.

And I had no clue what to order or how to eat it the way you were supposed to. My other concern was cost—Snuffy's was not cheap!

Fred looked at me, and said, "So, what are you going to have?"

"Oh, I guess a hot dog or a small hamburger."

God love him, Fred knew how nervous I was. It was one of the few times in my life that I was truly intimidated, and he knew it.

I needed some help.

Fred looked me in the eye, and said "I want you to have a big steak, and I am going to order it for you, okay?"

I replied, "Okay, Fred."

What a relief. I will never forget that moment of panic when I first looked at the menu, and had no idea what to do. It is funny, too, how the smallest things are those we fear the most.

Chapter Nineteen

The Korkers bought a summer home in Bayville, New Jersey, just south of Toms River and just before you get to Forked River. Fred owned his own business, which specialized in sheet metal fabrications, gold leaf work for churches, and unusual exhaust systems for restaurants. Actually, anything in metal, except cookie cutters, was Fred's business. The family was not really wealthy, but they were successful, and they made an above average living.

So now they now visited their dream summer home just about every weekend and although I was thrilled to be invited, I was still on the hook for the new car, additional insurance, and all the extra gas that I burned traveling around.

When I went to the shore and stayed with the family, Bette Ann and I were careful about not kissing in front of her parents. I was given a leather sofa to sleep on out on the closed patio while the family slept inside. I had no problem with this because as far as I was concerned, I was already in heaven.

My family, on the other hand, was not happy with my being away all the time.

Whenever I got back I went on work details, like hauling wood from empty lots and storing it in the cellar for the winter. Also loading and unloading coal for Uncle Vito. Our home was oil heated and there was a storage tank buried in the middle of the front yard and only the cap was exposed. The one rare time that my brother cut the grass while I was away, he hit the cap with the mower doing damage to it and the tank. That guaranteed that he would never do that chore again.

I had to scramble in order to live a normal social life with the Korkers and still do the work on Garfield Street. Sometimes it was done at crazy hours, like when I used the headlights of my Ford XL to finish mowing the yard.

Grandma Suzy did not care for Bette Ann. One day I drove up and left her in the car for a moment while I went to the back door to get a change of clothes.

Of course Suzy was there waiting for me.

"How come you're taking a whore around?" she said.

I answered, "My God, she is not whore, she is very nice. She's got a great family and I think she's the one I'm going to marry."

In Grandma's mind, a girl with blond hair had to be a prostitute.

I drove off that day, not really knowing how far Grandma would go to get what she wanted. Somehow, she found out who Bette Ann's mother was (probably from my brother), and Grandma telephoned her and said, "You'd better keep that daughter of yours away from my Franco or I will put a curse on you!"

Naturally, I did not know she had done this, and Bette Ann and I were driving to her house, and suddenly she asked, "How is it you go all the way around to the back door to enter your own home?"

I shook my head. How could I explain? There was so much she did not know about what my "home life" was really like. I resolved to tell her the whole thing, in detail. But not right then. So I said, "Hopefully you will understand when I tell you that my life is not like anyone else's that I know. I can't explain, Bette Ann, not at this moment. There are too many things going through my head. But I will, I promise."

When we got to the Korker's house, Mom let me know that Grandma had called. "What did she want?" I asked.

Mom glanced at Bette Ann, and then at me.

She said, "Your grandmother wants the relationship to end or she is going to put a curse on our family."

I went into a rage. I was so upset that I wanted to fly out of there and do something terrible to Grandma. How could she do this to me? How could she ruin my happiness because of some stupid ideas.

Amazingly, Mom seemed so cool about it. She said, "Franco, your grandmother is old and set in her old country ways. We understand that, and we love you for who you are. Don't worry about it."

How great it was to hear her say that! She was above all of the crazy stuff I had to put up with—the leaving of scissors under the baby's mattress so that when someone says "Your child is beautiful", the baby will not turn ugly. Grandma always kept an upside-down broom outside of the front door to ward off the evil thoughts of the neighbors. The idea was their bad thoughts would go to the broom and not the people in the house. You had to have a red bow over the front door on the inside of the house for good luck. You had to have a fig tree planted somewhere on the property, as that was good luck as well. If a pregnant woman cracked an egg with two yolks, that meant she was going to have twins. In Italy thirteen was lucky, seventeen was cursed.

A horn was also very lucky. The hand sign of little finger, index finger and thumb kept the evil eye away.

All of these strange things were normal to the older Italian people. Their beliefs went back hundreds of years, and there was no changing them overnight.

Anyway, the time had come for me to ask Fred for his daughter's hand.

Bette Ann, who was still in school, was due to graduate in June, 1965. This was towards the end of 1964, and if we were to have a June wedding after her graduation, we needed to announce our engagement. Standard etiquette required an engagement of at least six months.

Bette Ann was all for it, and so was I, but how would Fred take it?

We decided to tell Mom, and get her opinion on how to approach Fred.

She asked, "Don't you think you're too young to get married? What is the hurry?"

We explained how much in love we were and that we could do so much more being together. I went on to say, "My family's draining me of money and time and everything else. I don't know how much longer I can stay there after what Grandma did."

Mom understood, and she said, "Talk to Fred on Friday night. That way, most of the problems of work are behind him and he'll be more receptive, and have a lot more time to discuss it."

I think that Mom was just as nervous as we were when the night finally came. We were all in the kitchen having a cup of tea and talking small talk about the new cars coming out at American Motors. The new Rouge, the AMX, the Marlin.

Finally I worked up the courage to tell Fred how much I cared for his baby girl and how we deeply loved each other. I noticed that when I said the word love, he looked at Mom, and then he continued to stare at her while he listened to me.

When I finished speaking, I thought he was going to say something that I already knew—how he and Mom had married when she was only sixteen, and that it was not such a good idea to marry so young.

But instead, he studied me with his eyes, and said, "How will you maintain my daughter in the way that she is accustomed to living?"

I told him, "I don't know exactly. But I do know that I love her and that I will always work hard and be a good provider. I will do my best to keep her happy and see to it that she has all the finer things that we can afford, even though they may not be as much as what she has now."

"And when is this to happen?" he asked.

We both said, "We are hoping for June."

Then Fred got up from his chair. He had a tear in his eye and he suddenly gave me a huge hug that nearly cracked my ribs.

That night I went home and told my mother—not my grandmother as I knew what she would say. Mother cared more about my brother than she did about me. I was a provider for her, but nonetheless, a mother is a mother and I was still her son. I attempted to say all the right things and to remind her that I had done all the right things for them.

"I have to stop making so many payments. I need to save as much as I can for furniture and a down payment for an apartment, a honeymoon, and who knows what else."

That was as far as I got. She threw a fit!

"How can you do this to us? I came to America just because of you and now you leave me alone. You are ruining my life just to make yours a little better."

She went on and on.

When, finally, she paused to get a breath, I told her, "My whole life I lived more like a prisoner. I was never a son, nor part of this family. Since you don't care about my feelings, I can either move out tonight or stay until my wedding day and leave then.

"I'll continue paying as I have been, but don't expect any mowing or yard work or anything else because I won't have time to do it anymore. I need to start my own life."

Mother was quiet after that, but her eyes smoldered. She was angry and hurt, but mostly she felt cheated by the loss of future dollars and extra slave labor.

After that it took a long while for Suzy to look me in the eyes, but I figured that I had been more than a grandson to her. As for Mother, she forgave me. But she carried a look of resentment that lasted for at least another twenty years.

Chapter Twenty

Bette Ann and I arranged our wedding day with her parents and her sister Betty. Fred asked me what were we going to do about the engagement. I told him that I did want to get a nice ring although Bette Ann was not pushing for it. She did not want us to spend money we did not have. "I have friends in the jewelry business in New York City," Fred mentioned, "and they can help with a diamond that is affordable."

"I'll sell my boat," I said. It was the one I had bought when Fred and Mom got the house at the beach. We had had our fun with the boat, but now we had to set our priorities in order. Funny thing, once I made the move to sell it, I remembered how, one time, I had almost lost my life on account of it.

I had just gotten the boat, a thirteen-foot outboard boat powered by a Mercury thirty-five horsepower engine. It had a push button starter that was a big deal at the time and it was pretty darn quick. We set out one day, Bette Ann and I, to go crabbing. I used mullet for crab bait. I threw my line overboard and jiggled it slowly just above the sand bottom. This movement gave you the feel of the fish and it would alert you if a crab were to nibble at it.

Crabs are kind of stubborn. Once they start to eat something, they do not like to let go. As soon as you feel the tension of the crab eating, you must slowly pull up on the line, and up comes the crab. The trick is to get them just high enough to see them through the water, then come in fast with your net. Some people used traps but to me that was no challenge at all. After a short while I had a dozen blue claws that would make a super crab cocktail. The women loved it as I would cook and clean all the crabs and place the meat on top of a lettuce leaf that was layered into a dessert glass. The fresh crabmeat went on top. I offered separate mixes with varying degrees of hot sauce. Sometimes I set up the crab to dip into melted butter, too. Anyway, once I had a large enough supply of crabs, I pulled up the anchor and got ready to head back to Bayville and Sandpiper Beach where Mom's and Fred's summer home was.

I pumped the rubber plunger to get gas into the motor. Then I pushed on the chrome button to get the Mercury started. It groaned softly, would not start.

Holy smokes! We were two miles from the house and I had no paddles or oars. We were really out of luck. Bette Ann was happy to lie on the deck of the boat getting rays as I attempted to figure a way out of this mess.

I tried the starter a few more times, got even less of a response. So I figured that I would try to pull the boat to the house. Jumping into the shallow water, I felt the slimy bottom on the soles of my feet. I did not like it as just a few minutes ago I was getting good size crabs out of there and I also knew that there were snapping turtles where the lagoon came into the inlet. The water was dark—who knew what was down there.

So now I made sure that I floated, swam and doggy paddled, anything to avoid the bottom. I had about eight feet of rope and I did the old Tarzan trick of swimming and hauling. For the first forty yards the boat wiggled one way, then the other. It was fighting me. I finally got more into timing my strokes so that it wiggled a lot less and I made a lot more progress.

An hour or so into this wonderful exercise I could finally see the yellow house at the corner lot of Sand Piper Beach. It was still too far to yell for assistance, but I was at least getting somewhere. Of course in Bette Ann's mind everything was cool and I was her huff-and-puff hero.

Every now and then, I had to take a break. I just floated for a moment, then got going for another fifteen or twenty minutes of grueling exercise. Finally, as I got within one hundred yards of the house, I saw Fred, cigarette dangling from his bottom lip.

He smiled and kept on doing whatever he had set out to do. I cried out, "Hey, Fred. The boat broke down."

He went to the lower part of the dock, grabbed the rope and gave me some assistance. I was wiped, let me tell you. I felt like kissing the dumb dock.

So now Fred said, "What happened?"

"Well, I'm not sure. I guess the damn battery is weak or dead. Anyway, it wouldn't start."

Fred just looked at me strangely. Bette Ann got off the boat and Fred got on board and said to me, "Did you try this?" Suddenly the engine roared into action.

I was speechless for a moment. Then I said, "Fred, what did you do?"

"Just turned the key on and pulled the starting rope."

"I had no idea you could bypass the starter by pulling on that rope."

"Well, now you know."

So, many months later I was about to trade in my Tarzan memories for a diamond ring. Not a bad trade, the way I saw it.

Chapter Twenty-one

Before getting married, I decided to become a naturalized citizen. It was time.

The date for the wedding was set for June 25, 1965. Mom and Fred said that they would give us five thousand dollars or pay for the wedding itself. We went for the wedding. It did not need to be a huge one—just family.

Bette Ann and I went to Miron's furniture store in Plainfield and started a lay-a-way account. We found a beautiful Lane hope chest that we liked and a bedroom set with a carved headboard that we thought only movie stars had.

We were on our way.

One night when Fred came home and we were all around the kitchen table, he took out of his pocket a handful of diamonds and just slid them on the shiny tabletop.

He said, "My buddy let me take them home. You kids pick out the one you like. You said that your budget was five hundred for the boat, so all of those are about that price. The bigger ones are less clear and perfect and the smaller ones are better quality and more perfect. You guys decide."

We decided to go with the smaller, better quality diamonds, and Fred took them back. The ring setting was chosen by the women a little later.

They also loved picking out the dress, doing the invitations, and choosing the actual location of the wedding reception.

By now the kids in Bette Ann's class thought that she was pregnant since she had planned the wedding so close to graduation, but that was the furthest thing from the truth.

We were just being smart. We planned on having children when we could afford it.

My work was going well. I was the lead man on the order desk. I also won most of the promotional programs that American Motors sponsored. Plus I had a great relationship with all the dealers that contacted me. Due to my persuasive talents, they often stockpiled stuff before they were out of it. I would not accept any zero phone calls. Every one had to be a substantial order. Friendliness and knowing who I was talking to helped a lot.

It wasn't long before I received a huge promotion to warranty analyst for the entire zone area. Now I had my own personal office, a private secretary, and a few people working for me. Not bad for a twenty-year-old kid with a limited education and pretty average writing skills. All at once, I was making nearly seven thousand a year. You could buy a brand new Cadillac Eldorado for that amount of money.

The next hurdle was the fact that I was Catholic and Bette Ann's family was Lutheran. We needed to get married in a Catholic church. My church near my old elementary school was called the Little Flower Church. It was a tiny church, very pretty and the only church I had gone to in America.

We did some research about getting married at Little Flower. Once again Mary and Fred were so good about it. They said that Catholic and Lutheran were almost the same as far as they were concerned.

Having spoken to the Father at the church we learned that it was imperative that we take a course called Pre-Cana. This taught us about marriage and some of the things you should or should not do. Our first few classes were not bad as they informed you about this very serious step in life. Basically, the priest said that you were to treat your mate as you would treat yourself.

As time went on the six-week course got into child raising. The child had to be Catholic, well, no problem there. The priest said that if we did not want children right away, you had to practice the rhythm method. Using condoms was not permissible according to the church. Well, I certainly did not agree with that, and wanting to be extremely honest, I told Father that I did not agree with that, and until we could afford to have a family I would do my best to practice rhythm—but more than likely we would use some type of protection.

That did not go over very well. All of a sudden our six-week Pre-Cana became a two-month course with no graduation in sight. In each session we would go over many things and my honesty and openness would get me in heated battle with the Father not in a fighting way but him losing his patience with me and I could see that our date of June 26th was in jeopardy. Bette Ann and I, as well as Mom and Fred, had a long discussion and I finally said that my whole life I spoke to God and not through a third person. I said, "I want to continue that way."

The following session we talked to the Father and basically told him that we had changed our mind and that we would be starting a family as soon as God would allow it.

He said, "That is a wonderful idea!"

Then came the last session when you met with happily married people and learned from them how to be happy. We were so glad to be almost graduated, and to know that our wedding could go on as planned. When the final session arrived we were all set to say yes to everybody about everything. And we did, and that was the end of it. We passed, and now we had to do the invitation list.

My family was like a bunch of werewolves compared to Bette Ann's folks. I could not imagine them at a fancy get together, especially our wedding, which was going to be held at the Essex House in Newark, a pretty fancy place. Fred said his little girl was going to have all the right trimmings. He planned on rolling bars, champagne, no chicken but various well-planned courses.

No one on my side of the family owned a suit of any kind or shoes that were not for working with concrete. However, I was not going to think about that now.

We managed to get our list done and of course I made sure that I invited a few key people at American Motors as that was going to be the source of our life. We also planned to stay at the hotel the night of our ceremony, and the next morning we would leave for the Poconos to stay at Strickland's Resort for our honeymoon.

We had arranged to rent a cottage for the week. That was on us and we hoped that the Italian custom of providing cash in envelopes as a wedding gift was fully in force, as we had very little cash ourselves. We had done so much in such a short time.

Along with the wedding plans, I was also determined to become a naturalized citizen. When the time came I had Mom and her sister Betty accompany me for character witnesses. I also had to pass a very difficult oral test covering the laws and history of this great country of ours; and there was a written test as well. I can honestly say that the test that I passed in 1965 was so hard that most college kids would fail it today.

So I became Franco Antonetti, a very proud naturalized American citizen.

Now they say Italian-American, but I think that is completely incorrect. I am extremely proud of my heritage and certainly not ashamed of being Italian or I could easily have changed my name to Frank when I was swearing in. So it should be American-Italian.

Anyway, I was a citizen!

Chapter Twenty-two

Now we needed to find a place for us to live once we were married. Luck was on our side—new apartments were going up in North Plainfield, not very far from Fanwood and also very close to the Howard Johnson where we got our ice cream. The apartments were Cypress Gardens. Next door was a brand new Chevy dealer, HOB Chevrolet. We put down a deposit of one hundred and nineteen dollars for one month's rent, and after that, apartment eighty-five was ours. It was scheduled to be completed on June fifteenth.

Freddy arranged a bachelor's party at Snuffy's, the place where I had my first restaurant meal. There was a reception room upstairs that I never knew about. It was spacious and nice. Fred knew that the guys were going to have girls there or the normal stupid things guys do at affairs like this, so he decided not to attend, and to just let the fellows have their fun. I did not actually know about the party and it was a complete surprise to me when it happened.

The guys spent a fortune on this party. It was a buffet style dinner with shrimp, cold cuts, hot and cold Italian dishes, and of course, a lot of liquor. Although I was not quite twenty-one, I did my share of drinking one toast after another.

I still remember my embarrassment when they brought in two women that were paid to do exotic dancing. The idea was to get me excited in front of a crowd of well-wishing drunken friends. How could they imagine such a thing? That I would be turned on by doing a sexual act in front of a bunch of strangers? In front of my future brother in law and my Uncle Tony? Sex acts with strangers under a spotlight?

The whole thing made me uncomfortable. So I struggled through that weird part of the party, and then someone threw a shrimp at someone else, and a food fight started that seemed like a scene from *Animal House*. To me it was sad to see such a well-displayed buffet winging around the room, but that is what happened.

Well, that was my bachelor party, and I will never forget it.

Bette Ann graduated. Before we knew it, the day of our wedding was there and the Little Flower church was filled with lovely flowers that Mom had carefully picked for the occasion. We even had a stretch limo take us to the Essex House.

Freddy drove my XL so that we would have it for our trip to the Poconos. The reception was full of joy. The families were there and the folks from American Motors, and Uncle Vito had on a clean pair of shoes. His wife Aunt Judy was all smiles in her clean dress, that she borrowed, I am sure. My Uncle Joe shaved for the first time in probably a year. Aunt Ruthie was by his side, quiet as usual and looking lost in the crowd of strangers. My brother and his wife Roseann were somewhat more comfortable, but you could see that the wedding atmosphere was like something out of a movie to them and, no doubt, this just confirmed Aldo's idea of "Franco the Big Shot."

We did our dances, we had our many toasts. The bars were rolling, and God only knows what it cost Mom and Fred, but they really did it right. After having the cake that did not look real, as the two upper layers were being held up by white swans and on top was this lovely couple, a pretty blond woman and slender black-haired man.

The rum flavored cake was the customary cake for Italians; once again the Korkers obliged in providing every possible thing to make their second son feel the love that they had for him.

Each person who was invited to the reception had a specially picked favor that was also a swan on a tiny saucer that was filled with white almonds to confirm the purity in the marriage and covered to hold them in place by white lace. Fortunately the

Italian customs continued. The envelopes filled with money were presented to Bette Ann as we went around for our final good night before going to our hotel room.

Before leaving I saw Fred watching me take his daughter away. He was smiling, and I could see a tear in his eye. I thought to myself, "There is no way that I could ever do any more for my daughter if I was ever fortunate enough to have one."

As we entered the elevator Uncle Vito came up to us and in his sophisticated way, said, "Hey, do you need any rubbers?"

Bette Ann and I looked at each other and pretended that we did not hear a word he said. We just waved goodbye and the doors closed and the elevator whooshed us up to the tenth floor. Once we got to our room we found that Freddy had sent a special bottle of champagne. There were two glasses with the initial A on them.

As touching as that was, our mind was on the white bag that Bette Ann was holding. We got the envelopes out and threw them on the bed. Then we sat down and using hotel stationery, we wrote down the names and how much each person had given us, so we could thank them later. Then we calculated our total worth. Hopefully, it was going to cover our honeymoon.

I was surprised. The people that I was sure would give us something substantial, did not do so. But the ones who were not so rich gave us a lot more. The biggest disappointment was my mother. For years she had told me this story about how when my brother was married she gave him two thousand dollars, which was all the money he had ever given her. She had kept it for him because she knew he could not save it. When Aldo got married, she gave it back to him.

Well, I had given Mother thirty-five dollars a week for seven years. That came to over twelve thousand dollars, and on top of that, I gave her money whenever she needed it for water bills and all the rest. Sometimes I had to pay extra for using Suzy's radio, too. Or if I washed my car and used extra water—but who knows what I actually contributed altogether.

Anyway, her contribution to our marriage was fifty dollars. Not enough money, I thought, to cover my family's wedding dinner. Not to mention Grandfather's liquor bill and Uncle Vito's besides. They had sucked off a vat of wine worth well over fifty all by itself.

Oh well, as I would learn later on my mother thought I was the smart one in the family. Much smarter than my brother and that was her reason for giving me so little money that night. Yeah, sure.

Anyway, the honeymoon was terrific. We went off to the Poconos and at the resort we met some nice people who were also on their honeymoon. They did not have a cottage like we did, just a small room, so the four of us enjoyed the comforts of our cottage and its great fireplace, too.

The entire week went smoothly. The resort even had *bocce*, an Italian game that allows partners to throw clay balls toward a tiny ball in an effort to see who ends up closer once all eight balls are thrown. There were plenty of recreational activities—horseback riding, swimming, volleyball, badminton, horseshoes, etc. After a week of play, we left our cottage and came home to the new apartment that Mom and Aunt Betty had helped to set up. It was full of gifts for the newlyweds. We had already picked up our bed and hope chest at Miron's the week before. We added some little stuff and our dream apartment was furnished. There was a huge pool on the grounds and suddenly I realized that I was living the life I had always dreamed of. Meanwhile, I continued to do quite well at AMC and I did not quit the shoe store either.

Chapter Twenty-three

So I found a 1985 Rambler 990-H with a 327 engine that was in our inventory. The car had posi rear traction, bucket seats, power shift transmission, tinted windows, AC (very rare at that time) vinyl top (also rare) wire wheels, am/fm radio, speed control, power windows, power brakes, power side mirrors, power seats, power door locks, door edge guards, vent shades, door mats and power trunk release.

I probably left a few things off—but this was a machine.

Oh, yes—the dual headlights were vertical, also very cool looking.

This was really a "sleeper," a car that fools you. It looks normal but "jumps like a bunny," as we used to say.

At this time Bette Ann was spending a lot of time having coffee and tea with the girls (Mom and Aunt Betty) but she needed something to do. So she found work with a sales group as their "girl Friday" providing whatever was needed.

We got her a 1959 rambler classic 550 series. A very dependable 4-door car with the same engine as the 6 cylinder Jeep used.

Bette Ann worked for a few months. But the traffic on Route 22, a main NJ thoroughfare, got really heavy and her Rambler broke down one day and left her stranded. She called me and I came right away. There was smoke billowing out from under the hood. I took a quick look and saw that the engine was toast. Having friends in the business, I got the repair done at below normal cost, but the bill was a hit we did not need. We discussed the idea of her staying home. "What about raising a family?" I asked. "Are we ready for that?"

Bette Ann was as excited as I was, but she was also nervous about it.

"What if something should be wrong with the baby, what would we do?"

I went on and on about kids' names and the hundred or more boys in the Antonetti family. Well, maybe not hundreds, but I counted out the boys for Bette Ann.

"You have Uncle Joe who had Louie and Joe-Joe. You have Uncle Vito who has Joe, Frankie and Junior. You have Aldo who has Joey, Frank and Tommy. So, wouldn't it be nice if we had a little girl?"

Bette Ann nodded enthusiastically.

"I also would love to have a boy four years apart like you and your brother, so that if the kids want to go to college we can manage to afford it."

We must have been very fortunate because Bette Ann got pregnant quickly.

But she suffered through a hard summer; it was hot and she was uncomfortable much of the time. Luckily, we went to the Jersey shore on weekends. Fred had bought a twenty-eight foot Chris Craft with an inboard Oldsmobile V-8 engine. This thing was sweet and Fred would take us out and open her up. I mastered skiing in no time, and was doing tricks on one ski. I could handle sharp curves fifty-eight miles an hour with whip action speeds of eighty miles an hour. A few times I took some spills that ripped the bathing suit right off me. The hazards of the sport, I guess.

Believe it or not, I still attended my grandmother's Sunday dinners. Bette Ann came along, of course. My family was not that warm to her at first, but once she was pregnant they began to accept her as one of us.

On the 6th of October Bette Ann's time came, and we went to Plainfield Hospital around ten in the evening. You were allowed to be with your wife until she was moved to the delivery room. I placed a cube of ice on her lips, as I was told it would help. There were moments when she was in pain and she squirmed and nearly threw off her flimsy sheet. I had all I could do to keep her covered up in front of all the strangers that came and went in that part of the hospital.

I guess that she was in such pain that my attempt to keep her covered up was more of a nuisance to her than a help. So she told me, "I don't give a damn about that sheet."

Finally, it was time.

No one can tell you how you will feel at such a moment. I was praying, "Please, God, make it all be OK. It's not important if it's a boy or a girl, although I want a girl real bad. But really I just want everything to be OK and everyone in one piece after it is all over."

I kept praying and the waiting seemed to go on forever. Fred made it look like it was no big deal and even said, "Why don't we go have breakfast, she's not going to have that baby for hours."

Mom, on the other hand, was wringing her hands in a very noticeable nervous condition. She said, "Fred, I can't leave my baby's side even if it takes another twenty-four hours."

So we sat, slid, squirmed, stretched out on those hard leather chairs and couches until six AM. Fred had just gone to the coffee machine that we had visited at least a half dozen times already, and then, at 6:45, the doctor came in with the news—"You have a baby girl!"

As I write this today I can not help shedding a tear. The joy of those words still affect me so deeply. Yes, we had a little girl named Amie Marie. She was nineteen inches long and she was born on October 7th at 6:41 AM. As they wheeled Amie by us to clean her up, we were amazed by her beauty and her broad shoulders. My prayers had been answered. A healthy baby girl and Bette Ann was all right, too.

The phone calls were made to the world.

The Antonetti family of America finally had a girl child!

Chapter Twenty-four

My mother's first visit seemed amusing to us. We thought that she was being funny but I honestly think that she was serious. Although Amie's beautiful face clearly showed that she was a girl, Mother examined her to be certain. The custom at that time was to put infants in a cute little box that listed every detail about the baby. So when the time came to leave the hospital, you carried your baby out in that pretty box. I drove my Ambassador 990H to the front door of the hospital where Mom saw to it that her daughter sat in the front seat, and she gently gave Amie to her for the ride home.

In those days we were not concerned about seat belts—either that or we were just not thinking.

Our little apartment at 85 Cypress Gardens was bursting with friends and relatives, as this was a big celebration.

When I returned to work (and confirmed who the winner of the office pool was) I also informed everyone that my daughter's initials matched those of American Motors.

I was always gung ho, still am today.

It seemed that everything was going much too smoothly, so when I received a call that Grandpa was admitted to the hospital in Summit after having a heart attack, I began to prepare for problems. My superstitious mind said that things come in threes.

Grandpa had retired at seventy-five, but his heavy drinking and smoking had finally caught up with him. Fortunately, he pulled through OK. But now my mother needed to get a ride to work. My brother was not always willing to take her, nor did he go to work on a regular basis himself. So I decided as difficult as it might be— to teach my mother how to drive at the ripe age of 54. I also told her, "Since I'm going to teach you the physical part of driving as well as the rules, I might as well add one more thing to the lessons."

"What is that?" she asked.

"I am going to help you get your citizenship papers."

I think she was relieved to hear this, as maybe she thought I wanted to give her flying lessons as well.

In the end, it was easier—in spite of running over things—to teach my mom how to drive than it was to get her to pass her citizenship test. In those days you had to memorize a lot of stuff, but you also had to read and write, and she could do neither.

I took her to the test twice, and she failed both times. I never quit anything in my life, but after the second failure my mother gave up.

I then wrote to Florence Dwyer, the state representative, and complained.

I had taught my mother to read phonetically and to write, "I love America". She was a hard worker and a taxpayer, and she deserved to be a citizen.

Once again, after more preparation, we traveled to Newark and tried the test a third time. I said, "Mother, I am going to be right next to you at all times and do not worry and just listen to me no matter what."

She nodded. I could see that she was scared.

As luck would have it, she got a real taskmaster. This guy disliked foreigners, maybe Italians, in particular, and he was very harsh to her. Anyway, she passed a few questions with regard to law, but then the examiner demanded that she write a sentence.

Mother was all set to write I love America, when the guy blurted out something else, "The dog has fleas."

She had no idea what he said, what she should do. So she did not do anything.

At this point, he also asked me to leave the room. When I asked why, he answered curtly, "It's not customary for anyone other than the applicant to be present during the test."

I said, "I am her guardian and I have letters from our State Representative stating that I can be present and offer assistance, if necessary."

The man's face tightened, but he nodded when he saw the documents.

Then I told my mother to write, " I love America."

She began to write it in her very nervous and wiggily way. It was scrawled in bold letters and anyone could have read what it said.

Then the examiner said coldly, "That is not what I told her to write."

At this point I had nothing to lose so I told him, "Look, this woman has been in this country for over ten years. She's worked every single day of her life, paying taxes, and no burden to you or I, and, as a matter of fact, she helps many others who cannot work themselves due to age or infirmity. Her intention is to die in this country as an American citizen. By the way, I have more letters here from government officials who expect Mrs. Antonetti to become a naturalized citizen, and I intend to see that she becomes one."

While I went through this little speech, the examiner attempted to interrupt me a few times but I did not let him. When I was finished, he said, "You know how many people come to America and never learn to speak English?"

I shrugged. "Is that what makes them bad candidates for citizenship? Does that also affect their character? Does it make them bad people?"

He did not like hearing that, I can tell you. But suddenly he bent his head and banged his rubber stamp on my mother's paperwork.

It was something, seeing her with the rest of the people. She was waving an American flag as she was being sworn in.

I had to go through the same scenario for my brother, the prepping for the test and all of it, except Aldo got lucky with the examiner.

86

Grandpa recovered from his heart attack, but he still could not drive. So I decided that we needed to get mother a car. Well, the obvious choice was a Rambler, preferably a small one that was easy to handle and cheap to operate. We got a Rambler 220 at Stickel Motors in Springfield. The stories that I could tell about the trunk lids of that car are not believable. To be fair to my mother I will say that the trunk of the American Rambler 220 stuck out just a little more than the bumper did.

Apparently, Mother had difficulty turning her neck when she backed up and her way of knowing when to stop was when she hit something. Whenever I came over for Sunday dinner, the deck lid was freshly dented. I made arrangements to fix it (and pay for it of course) and my purpose was also to make sure our insurance agent did not see it. In those days it was common for the agent to come to the house to review the coverage and collect the premium.

This happened a number of times and each time, Mother explained that someone bumped into her from behind, I had it fixed and the agent never saw the damage. It went on like this forever.

Chapter Twenty-five

I would go to AMC and get home at about 5:45 depending how bad or good Route 22 was that particular evening and after changing and kissing the baby go to the shoe store and do my best to sell all I could, especially the slow movers. My life took a sudden change when I found out one day that AMC was closing down the New Jersey facility. They offered me a promotion at their Elmsford, NY plant, but we were so close to Mom and Fred and the family, and Bette and I did not want to move while Amie was so young.

Stickel Rambler hired me on immediately as a manager of their parts and service department, but that job did not look as good as another opportunity that presented itself. This was at Mack Boring, which sold rebuilt engines for cars, trucks and fork lifts. They had an opening for a counter person as well as an out-side salesperson. The salary was the same as the Stickel's position, so I took it. I had to learn all about the advantages of re-powering a school bus or a forklift, and for that matter, even a Mack truck.

A fortunate thing about my new employer was that they needed other workers, and I was able to get my old AMC buddy, George, a job there. George was thrilled to be a counter person and he was a very good worker, so this was good all the way around.

However, the job did not last long for either of us. The compensation package was not very good and working in Brooklyn, so far from home, was no fun at all. So, I quickly started to look elsewhere for work. As luck would have it, a friend told me about a possible job opening at Mack Truck in Somerville, NJ. This was right around the corner from where I lived in Plainfield, and I went there and applied for the job. The interview went well, as the V.P. of the company had read of my high school soccer and baseball career. We liked each other right away. But that did not get me the job.

Next I met with Mr. Bellamy, the warranty supervisor for the entire company.

We chatted a while and then he asked me what experience I had. I told him that I ran the warranty department for AMC all by myself and that I covered the entire region.

As it turned out Mack was just getting involved in the claims business and they were new at it. I could see that I probably knew more at that time than they did.

Mr. Bellamy seemed pleased with my background but he sent me up "upstairs" to the office of his boss, Mr. Spengler, a huge German who stood well over six-foot. He was a man who tolerated no nonsense and he spoke in very short sentences, asking me what I could do for Mack.

I gave him the same pitch I had given Mr. Spengler. He listened with a grave expression on his face, and to my surprise, he suddenly stood up, shook my hand and said, "You're hired."

The next thing I knew I had a new job with a starting salary of three hundred and fifteen dollars a month. The pay period was the first and fifteenth of every month.

I accepted and went home, happier than I had been in months. Here I had a job with a huge company close to my home, and I still had my second job, too.

The next day when I was to go for my physical in order to set up a starting date, I visited Mr. Spengler again. He was curious about why I was in to see him so soon after being hired.

I told him the straight truth. "Mr. Spengler, I appreciate your seeing me at this time and I know that I have not officially started but when I got home last night, I calculated the salary that we discussed."

Mr. Spengler's eyebrows raised when he heard the word salary.

I went on, "Well, I realized that I still need to work part time to make ends meet. If at all possible, could you justify an increase so I can quit my other job?" I said all of this in a hurry, and then there was nothing else to say.

He looked at me for a little while, but said nothing. Then with a slight smirk, he said, "No one's ever asked for a raise before they started to work."

I grinned, shrugged. "I'm the best at what I do, Mr. Spengler."

He seemed to really size me up then, and he said, "All right. Would an extra fifty dollars for each pay period work out for you?"

"You bet!"

We shook hands and I went out of his office to see the nurse about my physical.

So, now I was earning nine thousand dollars a year. With my part time work that I had no intention of quitting, I would earn at least another thousand. In 1965, a lot of college graduates were not making that much money.

I told Bette Ann and Mom and Fred and they all agreed that I was really one-of-a-kind, a world-beater, or something. Again we were living the life, and for newlyweds with a little baby girl less than a year old, we were very lucky.

The next thing I talked about with Bette Ann was getting our own home. She was amazed that we could talk it, let alone do it. But I scouted around and soon found a new house in Plainfield at 500 Church Place. The builder was a nice Italian guy who built only a few houses a year as a side job. We talked about his price for this one, and I asked what the price would be if he did not finish the upstairs. That would save a lot on the purchase price, I thought.

The style was a cute Cape Cod house and it was on a very tiny lot without a garage and actually without a backyard. The entire property was 100 feet wide and 40 feet deep. There was room for a driveway that did not have a garage and a small yard too. It had a basement, a side door and probably about 1100 to max 1200 square feet in total. I figured if I could afford it, then finishing the upstairs with two bedrooms would be easy for me—after helping Vito all those years, I knew how to build things.

Mom and Fred came over and looked at it and thought it was neat. But Fred asked, "how much?"

I said, "$16,200.00"

Then I told Fred that if he would lend me the $1,620.00 down payment, I would pay him back with interest in a very short time.

Fred said, "OK."

And then all hell broke loose.

The Plainfield race riots, lootings and burnings and violence of all kinds, started to happen. At our apartment we heard machine guns firing, sirens and it felt like there was a war going on—and there was.

We were worried about flying bullets. This was not an unreal concern. Police were on top of buildings in the shopping center near us. It was mayhem. Helicopter blades cut the air and we kept hearing them alter their pitch, rising and lowering in the night. What a time to have a baby girl. It reminded me of when I was very young or perhaps the stories I was told about farmers in Italy being strafed in their fields.

We were excused from work for the next two days. Those were the only days that I remember ever being off work other than for a vacation. In time, though, this dreadful nationwide disaster calmed down some, and we got back to some type of normal living.

On the news we saw where Newark, New Jersey and Watts, California were like war zones. There was not only shooting and looting but arson, too, huge fires that went on for blocks.

Not a very pretty time in anyone's life, but somehow we all got through it.

Chapter Twenty-six

We were fortunate because our new home was not affected by the riot, and as a matter of fact, was further from the heart of the problem than our apartment was. So it did not get destroyed by fire.

As soon as things quieted down, we closed the deal and we were in our new home by the time Bette Ann was twenty-one and I was twenty-three. At the same time Mom and Fred sold their home in Fanwood. They were spending a lot of time down at the shore, but they still needed a residence near Fred's shop in Jersey City. In the end they rented a nice apartment near us in Middlesex.

One day after going to work at the shoe store I spotted a cute toy poodle at a pet store in the Blue Star Shopping Center. I told Bette Ann about it and the next day we decided to get the little dog. We were given a warranty with her and we thought that we were really important having a dog with a special bloodline and a warranty. She was so tiny. We surprised Mom when we showed up with a toy poodle. She and Fred could not believe how little and cute she was.

"What's her name?" Fred asked.

In all of the excitement, we had not had time to think about a name.

I gave him a blank look and shrugged.

He said, "How about my mother's name, Fanny?"

"That's a perfect name," we agreed.

And from that moment on we had our little Fanny running around our new home and everywhere else we went. She was a pleasure and everyone —and I mean everyone—loved her.

My working hours lengthened, not only at Mack but at the shoe store and at home, too. After selling shoes until late in the day, I sometimes worked every night until two to three o clock in the morning installing vents, electrical fixtures, insulation, and what was required to frame out and finish our two bedrooms and the huge closet between them.

It probably took about two and a half months and hundreds of trips to hardware stores—these were the days before Home Depot. Anyway, we finally had enough money to pay Fred and Mom back. I personally knew that Fred would be insulted if I attempted to give him interest on his $1,620.00 loan, so I told Bette Ann that I was going to buy him a TV for the shore house patio. We gave Mom and Fred their loan in full with a big kiss and a Magnavox. Of course they told us that we did not have to do it. That is always what parents say, but I know that they respected us for it.

Just when everything was getting smooth, I got called for the draft. My duty as an American citizen was to serve and although it was not a good time for me, I had to ask myself—when is it a good time to be drafted? Anyway, I went to Newark and had my physical, and after that, you just had to wait it out. Would I, or would I not go to Vietnam? It was like the lottery—who knows?

At the same time, I became senior warranty analyst for Mack. Now I was responsible for all of the claims that pertained to fire trucks, off-highway vehicles, and all kinds of major component failures on Mack trucks. It was a full-time, full-throttle job and I took it seriously, and thrived on the responsibility. Our department was growing, so before too long, I got my old friend George a job at our department. This was without a doubt the best job he ever had in his life.

I was doing a lot of traveling for Mack. I visited local dealers to see first-hand some of the actual failures of their vehicles. This enabled me to respond more intelligently when I spoke to our vendors. At home, I had finished the upstairs and we all moved up there; Bette Ann and I in one room, Amie across from us in the other. The downstairs became the dining room, kitchen and living room, and what had been Amie's bedroom was a guest bedroom.

I managed to put up a white picket fence so Amie could play in safety, and things were pretty much perfect all the way around. I still visited my mother: Sunday dinner and, believe it or not, the irksome chores that had somehow always been a part of my life.

I had to abandon my own chores to come all the way to Berkeley Heights across the mountain from Plainfield. But I did not complain because in the back of my head was a plan, a dream, an idea that had lodged itself so deep I could not get rid of it if I wanted to. That dream was to be the president of Mack Trucks. Seriously, the dream was real. And that was where I was headed.

Chapter Twenty-seven

When we drove to Mom's, or anywhere else for that matter, I would point out to Amie and Bette Ann every Mack that was coming or going. My brother at this time still had no real job as he worked piece work at McGregors and made a fair living but had no insurance and would not think of getting any. Never a thought about retirement either. Basically, he lived from day to day. He used to say to me, "Hey, how does it feel to be a big shot?"

That was how he saw me, I suppose. Not that I worked hard and had two or three jobs. Not that I was hungry for the finer things in life, no, just that I thought of myself as a big shot. I had to remind him that whatever I did, it was to make myself a better provider. One job that Aldo did not know about was when I worked with a caterer named Chet. This was weekend work, squeezed in between shoe-selling, house-fixing and other things. Our job was to set up and cook specialty items, anything from hamburgers to oysters, and I was paid anywhere from thirty to fifty dollars for the day plus we took home roasts and hams and other food that was not used. All of this helped us reduce our cost of living, and I was thankful for it.

One special event I remember well was Somerville Inn's New Year's party. Bette Ann was excited about this because it cost eighty dollars a couple, which was way beyond our means. I told her that I just had to do a little work for Chet and then the evening was ours.

Well, the real truth was that we were catering that night. Bette Ann made mashed potatoes in a huge pot. She was stirring the pot with what looked like an oar and serving a huge number of people in a beautiful dress covered by a dirty apron. But our time finally came, and we got to eat and celebrate and watch the hour click over to the next year. We made fifty dollars each, Bette and I. But I had to put up with her making fun of me for having invited her to that "gala affair" in the sweaty kitchen.

One day I got tired of Aldo calling me "big shot" and I asked him if he wanted to work at Mack himself. As much as I really did not care for him as a person, I accepted responsibility for him as my somewhat helpless brother. He responded as I figured he would, feeling sorry for himself. "I can't read English too good," he said. "I can't even fill out an application."

"Well, seeing as how I'm a big shot, I know some people who don't care what you can read or write as long as you can be a parts picker. However, I do not want to be embarrassed, as my entire future is Mack. So if you work there, you've got to be a regular worker, not just when you feel like it."

Aldo's face brightened. "I would never embarrass you," he said, and I felt he really meant it, and before long he was working at Mack, too. He would be in the warehouse while 'The Big Shot' was upstairs in the office. But every so often I had to go to our Hagerstown facility in Maryland. The private helicopter picked me up in front of the building, and later that same afternoon, I returned. I could imagine what my brother must have felt when his coworkers told him that they saw his younger brother take off in the Mack private copter.

Pennsylvania

Chapter Twenty-eight

My brother was on his way. He had insurance for the first time in his life, and his kids were getting proper medical treatment. His wife also had medical attention that she desperately needed at that time. But, you know, Aldo never said anything to me about how thankful he was for any of it.

One day the word came down that Mack was going to have a brand new executive office. This was to be a six story building in Allentown, Pennsylvania, "the truck capitol of the world". Allentown was where all Macks were made and it seemed a million miles away but actually if you stayed on Route 22 west for about sixty to ninety minutes you were there.

I confirmed my position at Mack—they loved me.

So I figured the smart thing to do was to jump the gun and move before everyone else did. And by the time the new executive office was finished, we would be in Allentown in a new house.

This move was going to be a little more difficult for Mom. She would really miss us. As for my family, well, I thought it would be easier on me as I would have no more yard work, house painting and gardening. It would be worth it to me to give my mother some money rather than drive three hours to do it myself.

We picked out a lot and decided on a tri-level home that had three bedrooms, a huge family room, living room, fireplace, kitchen, two full bathrooms. The spacious house was on a large lot. I had always wanted to live on top of a hill, and this house was situated that way. If there was any fault in the place it was the single car garage. However, coming from no garage, I could live with that. We actually had the house finished just before ours sold, but Mack took care of the funds through a bridge loan that basically lent you money for a short period of time at low rates until your sale went through. Our new home was $23,500.00 and we sold our little palace in Plainfield for $22,400.00 We made a great profit and it seemed like we made a jump from a comfortable home to a dream house overnight.

Finally we had our gorgeous executive office that still stands today at Mack Boulevard. It has a huge three-story bulldog statue attached to the front. Our department expected and received a lot of respect.

The building was well appointed—a rotunda meeting room for international affairs. This was a massive room made up of rich wood and furnishings. The lobby was stained wood with thirty-foot ceilings. There was a globe featuring the locations of dealers worldwide. Extremely impressive to me since I wanted it to be at the top of the globe myself. To get more in sync with the organization, I got a Johnson CB that was like a phone. My new car at this time was a 1968 Cadillac convertible with a specially installed gold bulldog on the hood. We actually bought this car to replace Bette Ann's Rambler, which Freddy totaled one night at a party. The strange thing was he never said so much as sorry. But then I have bad luck with brothers, don't I?

The license plate of the Caddy said in solid chrome, BULL-DOG I.

My phone had the same handle. When I was on the road I spoke to the truckers, "Bulldog One, come in!"

Chapter Twenty-nine

Bette Ann thought I was a little loony, but then she had known that from when she first met me. I was a company man, through and through. I went so far as to have Mack hats in my trunk. I got these from our novelty department. I could write them off, too, as they were a company expense, the way I viewed it. I talked to Mack truckers on the highway and sometimes I asked them to pull over and I would give them a free hat.

They loved this! You would hear them talking about it on their CB for the rest of their trip.

So, everything was working out for us in Allentown except I was missing my extra jobs. We had a cool neighborhood, mostly young families with small children. A good place to raise kids. I found an ice skating rink in town and they had skating sessions with very little discipline and low turn out. I spoke to the owner and let him know that I had run the big rink in Berkeley Heights.

I said, "You know, I could do a good job for you and get your attendance up. Parents of young children aren't going to bring their kids here because the discipline is so slack." I let him take this in for a moment.

The owner, a tall narrow-eyed man, looked me over, saw that I meant business and replied, "What would you do about it?"

I told him, "I would need at least thirty dollars a session, plus my family would skate free whenever I was at work."

"What's that going to do for me?" He looked at me uneasily.

"You'll see," I said, "I will bring in people. This place is going to be packed."

He thought about that, then said, "You're asking too much for your services. I can't afford that much."

"OK. I'll do it for twenty a session, but if I manage to get some teams to skate after the sessions, you'll give me the ten dollar difference. Is that all right?"

The owner lit a cigarette, and blew some smoke into the air. What he did not know was that I had already made contacts—teams that wanted a place to practice from midnight until two. They would pay a lot more than he could make in a session plus they would be less problematic than little kids. Also they would use the facility's sharpening services for their blades.

At last, the owner took me on, and I started work immediately.

From the start—as soon as I got the word out—the rink was a hit. Both with families early in the evening and with the ice hockey teams later on. It worked like a charm and some nights I earned sixty dollars for working two sessions and making ice for the league practice. Sometimes I came home at two in the morning still shivering from the thirty-eight to forty-five degree ice rink. I hopped into bed for less than three hours of sleep, and then I was back at Mack. But I have to say I loved every minute of it.

Jim Carnevale lived in the biggest house in the sub-division. It was right across the street from us. He was much older than we were and he and his wife Ruth had the finest of everything. Jim was a nice guy but he had a lot of hang-ups. His two daughters were not allowed to sunbathe on the grass as it would cause the grass to be squashed and when they would get up it would not match the rest of the yard. He would then have to comb the grass with a rake so it would look perfect. He had a brand new Chrysler 300 and once his wife had to borrow it to do an errand. When she got back Jim was very upset with her said she could never drive it again.

I thought that possibly she banged it up or spilled juice or coffee in it or something like that and knowing what a fanatic he was I could almost understand his frustration. He called over to his house, grabbed me by my left arm and said, "Frank." (I hated that he called me Frank instead of Franco.) But since Jim was an older man and so set in his ways, I let him call me what he wanted to.

"Look at this!" he said when he showed me his car. He pointed to the back seat.

I looked for what seemed eternity and could not see anything unusual.

I said to him, "What's wrong?"

He replied, "Can't you see the belts?"

"What belts?"

"The rear seat belts—they're all bundled up instead of being aligned on the seat and hanging down the way I left them."

Can you imagine being that upset over nothing? Well, that was Jim. One day he came over and told me that I needed to paint the mortar between my bricks in front of the house. He bitched over this, but he was nice enough to help me with the work so it was hard to say no to him. Another time he came over to inform me that from his kitchen he could see that my metal gutter between the two roofs on top of my house was rusting a little.

"You should get up there and paint that. People will think you are slobs."

I did it just to keep him happy, and it did. The next thing I knew he wanted to help us put in our first in-ground pool. Jim was worth his weight in gold, but you had to overlook his eccentricities, which were many and varied.

Chapter Thirty

In the spring of 1970 I worked harder at Mack than ever before. I would catch the President once in a while in the elevator as he was going to the top to the sixth floor and me to the fourth, and he would say "Good to see you in early." I was always thrilled to have him speak to me as he indulged in very little small talk.

One day I was invited by one of our vendors to play golf at the club. I had played golf a little with some friends in New Jersey and typically they would criticize me as my stance was wrong, the way I held the club was ridiculous, and my clubs were ancient. Mostly, I just felt lucky to shoot par and to occasionally get a few birdies. Anyway, this time we met at the Lehigh Valley Country Club.

This was a big deal to me and I wanted to make sure that I was not intimidated by the game. I tended to be loud especially if I hit a good shot or sunk a long putt. I was, however, just as excited when one of the others did a great shot. Thank God, I was shooting a respectable round when the conversation started to get murky.

Two of the guys were complaining about the union. The problem with this country, they said, was that workers did not make enough money and did not get enough time off. Although it may not have been good etiquette, I finally put my two cents worth into the mix. "I don't get it! Here we are playing this unbelievable course that most people would give their right nut to play and we're playing for nothing—no, it's better than that, we are being paid to play here—and you guys are bitching! I think that we are the luckiest people in the world and Mack is the greatest company in the world, and if you guys really feel that Mack sucks or does not have enough benefits, why don't you guys leave?"

They looked sheepish after that, I can tell you. After a little silence, they sort of apologized. We finished the round and I excused myself from going into the clubhouse for refreshments, as they were about to do. I felt a bit guilty for sounding off like that. Maybe I should have been more diplomatic. But the thing was, they hit a subject that was close to my heart. Mack.

I told Bette Ann what happened that night. I said I was somewhat worried about what those guys might say about me. I did not really know them that well, and it's easy to spread rumors in a company like ours. Bette Ann listened and said, "You said the right thing. Besides, what's done is done."

A few days went by and nothing happened. Then I heard from my boss, Mr. Spengler. He said I was supposed to go up to the sixth floor to see Mr. Z.C.R. Hansen at 9:00 AM. Can you imagine what was going on in my mind? I asked around our department to see if anyone from there had ever been called up to see Mr. Hansen, and they said no. Time moved so slowly. I looked at the clock and it was one of those clocks that the minute hand ticked loudly. It was 8:19, and 8:20 ticked about an hour later.

Finally, I could not wait any longer. I got in the elevator and took the dismal ride up to floor level six to face my punishment.

On the sixth floor I passed by the brass helm wheel—Mr. Hansen's way of saying that he was running the ship. I walked up to one of his private secretaries.

"Franco Antonetti to see Mr. Hansen, by appointment."

She gave me a brief, but quickly fading smile. "I am aware of the appointment," she said. "Mr. Hansen will see you in a few moments."

I sat in a plush leather chair, and waited. Then after a few more minutes, the secretary escorted me into an office that was larger than the top floor of my new home. Behind a great brown mahogany desk flanked by numerous Mack bulldogs there was a brass plaque, The President.

The first thing that came to my mind when I saw Mr. Hansen, face to face, was that he had the widening jaws of a bulldog himself.

But now he got up from his chair and offered me his hand. "Sit down, and relax," he growled.

Can you imagine trying to relax in this situation?

Then the next thing that happened was there was a lot of noise out in the reception room. The door opened and in walked a camera guy and with him was a man speaking into a microphone.

"Is this the gentleman you were talking about Mr. Hansen?"

Mr. Hansen nodded. "This is Franco, the young man I wanted you to meet. This country needs more good, honest workers like Franco, but I am afraid he may be one of a kind." Mr. Hansen smiled and the microphone guy laughed.

All the while, the video camera was rolling and then I was being asked a bunch of questions by the man with the mike, who, as it turned out was a TV newsman.

"How did you come to America?" he asked.

Puzzled, I found my voice, and began to tell my story, little by little. The whole time I was talking, though, I was asking myself, "Why is this happening to me?"

It took about fifteen minutes for the questions and answers to conclude, and then, as briskly as they had entered, the newsmen departed.

Mr. Hansen then explained why he had summoned the news people to Mack to interview me. Apparently, he had heard about how I had blown off steam at the golf course, and told those guys off. What he heard, he liked.

"I like a young man who knows where he is going, Franco. But I admire him even more when he is not afraid to speak up for what he believes in, and when that belief is Mack, then I have nothing but admiration for him. Do you follow what I am saying?"

I nodded. I was hardly able to speak.

When I left his office he clapped me on the back and said, "I am going to see a lot more of you around here, Franco."

The evening newspaper ran a full-page article on Franco Antonetti. There was a big picture of Mr. Hansen and me in his office standing in front of an American Flag.

A PROUD AMERICAN, the headline read. In addition, "The Mack News" had a full story, too, and it was even better than the local paper's tribute. Mr. Hansen sent some gifts to Amie, too. A large stuffed toy bulldog, cups and towels and clothes, and all of them with the Mack logo.

In the next few days I got calls from everyone I had ever met in Allentown. This great and magical meeting with Mr. Hansen increased my bond with the Bulldog. And it confirmed my dream of wanting to be just like him.

At home when Bette Ann and I discussed destiny and how things unfold we looked back on some of the decisions we had made, and we were extremely thankful that someone was looking after us. We also realized that this would not be a bad time to start thinking about a second child.

And so, it was not long before we found out that Bette Ann was pregnant and again we were blessed. Life had never been better.

Chapter Thirty-one

We were at the shore one weekend and Bette Ann was about three months into her pregnancy. One morning she looked pale and started talking to Mom very quietly, and the next thing I knew they were calling an ambulance. Fred and I did not know what was going on. Both Mom and Bette Ann were crying. Finally, Mom said, "She is bleeding a little, so we're going to have her checked out at the hospital at Tom's River."

The ambulance came, and Mom and Bette Ann went together.

I got in the Caddy and followed the ambulance. Fred was with me.

By the time we got to the emergency room, we found out that Bette Ann had already been examined. A doctor told us that it looked like we were going to lose our boy, but they were trying to stabilize Bette Ann, and we should hope for the best.

I asked the doctor, "Is there any way to save my son?"

"Do you want us to?"

I could not understand why he said that.

"Of course!" I shouted.

The doctor looked surprised. Maybe he was under the impression that we were newlyweds and it would be OK to let the miscarriage happen, let nature take its course.

I said, "My God, no, I want my baby. Please do all that you can to save him."

I still am not sure why his reaction was so strange.

So, anyway, Bette Ann was given injections to help her hold the baby. For the next forty-eight hours, she was under a close watch, then she was released but she was not to do anything physical. The family stayed with Mom at the shore for two weeks.

I drove home and worked during the week and came down each weekend. The following Friday, when I arrived, I found out that Fanny was soon to have babies of her own. She had mated with a pedigreed poodle, and on Saturday morning, I heard some squeaking. It was Fanny. I rubbed her tummy as she lay on the bed, and she gave birth to four cute little pups. One looked like her and another was chocolate in color and very pretty. Not knowing anything about delivery of doggies, I just kept massaging Fanny's tummy, and more pups kept coming. This dog adventure that had such a nice ending made me feel that it was a good omen.

However, some time after this a friend of Fred's was stranded in his boat out on the bay. The guy had only one arm, and we went out there to rescue him.

We cranked the big engine of the Chris Craft, and went off to find Lefty. A cold winter wind was blowing. With the speed of the boat, the wind went right through you.

We were twenty minutes out when the weather really worsened. By this time Fred was saying, "He must've got back in somehow. He's not where he said he'd be." Fred was set on going back home in the next few minutes if we did not see him.

Then we saw Lefty's boat anchored about 100 yards from shore. There was nothing but empty land where he was moored, a desolate place. When we came up to Lefty's boat, Fred said, "Hang on, we'll be alongside in a minute."

It was good to see the man was OK. If he had stayed overnight, he would have ended up frozen.

"I'm not leaving my boat," Lefty said.

Meanwhile, Fred idled his engine, and called out to Lefty, "If you don't jump in this boat we are leaving."

With that, Fred's prop got tangled with Lefty's anchor rope. In another half-second we were stalled. We were about twenty feet away from Lefty's boat and Fred was fuming. He told me to jump overboard and see how bad the rope was wrapped around the prop. I was freezing already, but I took my sneakers and socks off and emptied my wallet and change and jumped into the water. You have absolutely no idea the feeling you get from frigid water unless you have been in it yourself.

It was like needles and knives going into your skin, and worse, I had to go underwater, too. The salt was burning my eyes and my hands were too cold to feel the prop very well. Plus there was the violent motion from the waves moving me back and forth. The suction from the boat and the action of the waves shoved me hard against the stern. My knee got banged pretty good, but at the same time, I got my hands around the rope that was tangled around the prop shaft. It had tightened so much that I could not do anything to loosen it, even if it was out of the water, which it was not.

I told Fred, "It's too tight, I can't budge it."

"For Christ Sake, get out I'll do it!"

"Fred it's stuck, give me a knife or something and I'll try to cut it loose."

There were plenty of fishing knifes in the Chris Craft, and he got me one, and after a half a dozen tries I got the rope cut.

I jumped back into the boat; there was no way I could stay in any longer. Fred put the boat in neutral, and started the engine. It caught right away. Then he put it in gear. The boat vibrated to all hell and it was obvious that we were going to tear something up if we kept it running any longer. Obviously there was still some rope wrapped around the prop. Fred said, "You have to get a little more off."

I looked at him as if he was crazy, but I jumped back in anyway. The misery returned one hundredfold. This time I was more shivery, and I could not keep my hands in place or make them do what my mind told them to do.

Still, I managed to free the prop again.

We attempted to go and the vibration was much less.

Lefty by this time had jumped ship and was in the Chris Craft, safe and sound, but I was a chattering wreck. We strained against the current and wind, both of which were against us. The engine was struggling and at this speed it was going to be hours before we got home.

Once again, a familiar feeling came over me. It was the same feeling I had had many times before in my life. I knew that I would die.

Actually, I had to go into the drink two more times to fix the prop. In the end, we were going at about the speed of a fast swimmer. We were, however, moving forward, not being pulled away from the shore.

"Get down in the hold, get your wet clothes off and put on my windbreaker," Fred ordered. I was in this compartment, two feet by two feet with the cover over my head, out of the wind, but also out of my mind. I was in deep trouble. I was frozen stiff, and could not feel my limbs very well. I was sure I was going to die. But I talked myself into believing that I could live if I could only count up to 1,000. I knew if I tried real hard I could do it, so I started counting.

One, two, three . . .after what seemed forever, my count reached 865.

I heard Fred yell to Mom, "Mary get a hot tub going for Franco, right away!"

The boat banged against the side of the dock. Fred and Lefty helped me out of the compartment. I could not walk without help. Mom made me a pitcher of Manhattans and I do not recall exactly how much I drank or how long I sat in the tub with Bette Ann looking after me. It took hours for the shivering to go away. And then I felt numb all over but maybe that was the Manhattans.

I did not die. For some unexplainable reason, I did not even get a cold or any bad side effects. The next morning I woke up good as new.

The grim reaper had missed another chance.

Chapter Thirty-two

We received our first indication on March 3rd at about five in the afternoon that this could be the day for our son to arrive. Since we had a bit of snow on the ground and a possibility of more coming, I felt to be safe that I would go to Allentown Hospital early.

Since we were without any family close by it was just us this time. I was nervous because we had been told that the shots Bette Ann had taken to avoid the miscarriage could affect the baby. We could have complications—who knows, a malformed child. We said no matter what comes we will love this baby. But the honest truth is no one really knows how they will act until it happens. The thing to do was to pray for the best possible outcome.

It was three hours after I registered before they took her to the prep room. It was going a lot faster than when we had Amie. But every time is different. I chose not to call anyone because they could not do a thing being so far away. I also didn't want them to drive all the way to Allentown in a snowstorm and who knows what could happen. I think that I was correct just to handle it alone and once I knew good or bad I would let everyone know.

At just about 10:00 PM the doctor started to come up the hallway towards me. The hallway seemed like a tunnel and his walk appeared to be in slow motion and for some reason I was judging his facial expression as a sign of a problem and not fatigue or anything else. I could hear my own heart beat with each step toward me. I was half-sitting and half-standing getting ready to greet the doctor.

"You have a son," the doctor said. "He was born at 9:50."

"Doc, is he OK?"

With a little hesitation, he replied, "Yes, but...."

I felt weak, afraid for him to finish his sentence.

"Your son has a hydrocele," he continued.

I had no clue what that was.

The doctor proceeded to explain.

"When the testicles drop at birth, the opening where they drop from inside the sack should close, but sometimes it does not. This causes liquid from the body to travel in and out of that area and usually when a baby cries it makes more liquid and the testicles enlarge till the liquid escapes back from where it came from."

"What should we do about this problem?" I asked him.

"Many times it cures itself. If not, we'll operate."

I saw my son through the window where they clean up the babies and dress them.

As the nurse was washing my son it was obvious that his testicles were not normal. They were the size of a bull's. She looked back at the window where I had been glued. She motioned to me, and said, "Is this your boy?" I gave her thumbs up confirming that those award-winning balls were from my family line. Now I went to see Bette Ann and found out that she went through a difficult birth as our son was 8 pounds 15 ounces and was 21 inches long. She was groggy but awake.

She whispered, "How's the baby?"

I cheerfully told her, "He's a beautiful baby and I know he's my son as he has my balls."

At that time she had no idea about what I was talking about but she smiled anyway and said not to make her laugh, she was in too much pain. I kissed her and excused myself. I had so many calls to make.

The first call was to Mom. I know that I probably should have called my mother but my heart said that Mom would really want to know and my mother could care less.

I caught Mom having her usual cup of tea. As I started to tell her I got all choked up and like a little kid I could hardly get the words out that I had a son.

She screamed "Fred! They had the baby!"

Then came all the usual questions. When did you go to the hospital? How long did it take? Why didn't you call us? How big, how long, and on and on.

I cut to the quick. "We have healthy boy with very big balls."

Now, my wife's skin was very light. She was an extremely beautiful woman with dark brown eyes and sandy blond hair. Amie also had fair skin but probably not as fair as her mom's. She had blue eyes and very little hair at birth.

Our son, whom we had decided to call Franco, was Buddy—that is, Buddy was his nickname, and it stuck. A friend of mine in school was named Anthony and his nickname was Buddy and I always liked that and it stayed in my mind that someday I would have a son named Buddy.

Well, Buddy was a little more like me as his skin was fair but in between his sister and me. He had plenty of hair and blue eyes. Just like me. In fact, when I looked at him I saw little Franco in Rome in 1945.

Allentown was full of Pennsylvania Dutch people. Our nurse was one of those women, heavy set and strong. Before Buddy and Bette Ann could leave the hospital, I had to answer a bunch of questions. The big Dutch nurse had a clipboard, and she kept glancing at my wife and then at Buddy and with a sincere face she asks Bette Ann, "Are I-talians considered white? They are, aren't they?"

Bette Ann looked at me and then at the nurse. "I hope you are kidding!"

The nurse blushed. Obviously, she was not kidding.

Well, we left Allentown Hospital and now we were off to Wescosville.

Jeff, a friend of mine that worked at Mack was a gifted artist and he offered to decorate Buddy's room with an American Revolutionary theme. He drew soldiers that were about three feet tall on the walls as well as cannons and drums and flags. He did such a beautiful job that I wanted to continue the theme by building Buddy a wagon for his bed. Although we had his crib in our room we continued fixing up his room as if he were already a little boy.

Amie had her own room and I drew a beautiful rainbow on her back wall.

I also installed a pull down ladder so that in the center of our hallway you could go into the attic that I had converted into Amie's playhouse. She had so many toys up there it is a wonder that it did not buckle the ceiling.

With all the things that were going on, it is a wonder that I got everything done. Fortunately I don't require more than four or five hours of sleep. I am a machine that jumps to attention first thing in themorning and I run all day without rest.

I completed a lot of projects with very little money while we lived in Wescosville. I always looked for deals, and one of the very best was a used above ground swimming pool. I found one that was available in Gillette, New Jersey. All that was needed was to come over, empty it out, dismantle it and take it away. I transported it to my home in Pennsylvania with the help of my old friend George from AMC.

Then I cleared a thousand wheelbarrows of dirt, which, in turn, became fill for landscaping projects around the house. Before long I had water running in the liner and our pool was a reality. Next I built a deck with a gate at the top of the stairway for safety.

It looked good when it was done, and my neighbor Jim Carnevale had little to say about it. And that was saying a lot.

After the pool was finished, I planted trees in beautiful rows and landscaped the whole property so it looked like the Garden of Eden. The last major project in the back yard was done with the help of Fred. We built the cutest playhouse close to the pool. It was large enough, in fact, to be a changing room. It looked exactly like a miniature of our house complete with tiled ceiling and floor.

One day I overheard some neighbors talking about all the upgrades on the place. They were saying that "He must be one rich guy to afford all those fine things he's got." I had to chuckle at that. The neighbors considered us as the rich people even though they were probably a lot richer than we were.

But what is rich anyway, if not talent, initiative, and energy. And utilizing the gifts that God has given you. In my case, He gave me the ability to make anything I wanted to. It did not occur to me back then that I was following the same path that my hard-nosed Grandma Suzy had set me upon when I was a little boy in Berkeley Heights.

Top left – My Mother's Chiosco

Top right – Me over the Tiber River

Middle left – At the ocean in Ostia, Italy: Annita on left, Mother on the right, Mafalda in the middle and me in front

Bottom, from left to right – Eldest sister Maria, Mother, Dad, Aldo, Ofelia, and Franco

Top left ~ Franco at 4 1/2; Top right ~ Me and my Mother
Middle right ~ Aldo, Franco & Carlo
Bottom left ~ Carlo & Me; Bottom right ~ Franco & Aldo

GOVERNOR LIVINGSTON REGIONAL H. S.
UNION COUNTY CHAMPIONS
1961

*Top - 1961-Governor Livingston Regional High School
County Champs... "I'm in the 2nd row, 7th from left;
Curt is in the back row, far right."*

*Middle left - Aldo & Franco: "What I wore when I first
arrived... the sausage pants"*

Middle right - "School days in my '57 Buick"

Bottom left - Me, Grandma Suzy, Mother in New Jersey

Top – Columbia School 8th Grade Graduation...
"I'm in the top row, 9th from left"

Middle left – Soccer Champs: 1962

Middle right – GLRHS: "I kicked!"

Bottom left – "Sports gave me strength and all the medals"

Top - "Our first house in Plainfield, NJ"; Middle left - "My sister came to Berkeley Heights to visit" (Aldo, Ofelia, Franco); Middle right - "Amie, Bud & Me with Cousin Tod at Wildwood"; Bottom left - House at Wescosville, PA.

M4690-52 500 Church Pl. Plfd.

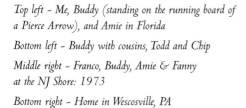

Top left - Me, Buddy (standing on the running board of a Pierce Arrow), and Amie in Florida

Bottom left - Buddy with cousins, Todd and Chip

Middle right - Franco, Buddy, Amie & Fanny at the NJ Shore: 1973

Bottom right - Home in Wescosville, PA

Top right - Buddy & Me: Stone Mountain, GA "Yard of the Month"

Middle left - Amie & best friend Beth in PA

Middle right - The blue Mercedes SL

Bottom left - "New Mack Mid-liner Team...1980 Regional Guy"

Bottom right - Open House at new Mack facility in Richmond, VA

Top - Bette Ann & Amie in front of our new home in San Ramon, 1982

Middle left - Amie & Buddy with new Caddy and Mercedes, San Ramon, 1982

Middle right - Me at a driving range in San Ramon, CA, 1983

Bottom right- Buddy & Me at the driving range in San Ramon

Bottom left - Truck parade for Buddy at Bollinger Canyon School, San Ramon

Top left - Mack Truck show in Chicago... they hired models io interest guests into viewing the product

Top right - Mack group attending the sales meeting in San Francisco just before I learned that our division was shutting down

Middle left - "Tall girls at the Mack show"

Bottom left - "My Mercedes & Me in the Redwoods"

Bottom right - On a Mack cruise in 1986

Top left - Amie in Oakland at the Mack dealership I ran, and the Bulldog I had painted at the service entrance...
"Welcome to Bulldog Country"

Top right - Mack Oakland—1983

Middle left - Awards at the Factory Store, Oakland, 1983

Middle right - "My toys!"

Bottom left -"The Jeep I rolled and almost died in"

Bottom right - "My 45th birthday," 1989

Top left - "My retirement party—they gave me a Wal-Mart vest"

Top right - Surprise 50th

Middle left & right - "My new life—98..." Teri and Me, Buddy & Me

Bottom left - Franco & Teri "Visiting Rome after 45 years"

Bottom right - "My old apartment on the 3rd floor"

Top right – Raymond Dealer meeting

Middle left – Another one of my toys

Middle right – Buddy & Amie in 2002 at our home in Gilbert, AZ

Bottom – The Zimmer

Chapter Thirty-three

My life changed again when I met Mr. Schaller, an extremely well-educated executive who was in charge of Mack's Off-Highway division. Mack produced a highway truck just like the Peterbilt you see today. Their refuse trucks dominated the market. They also produced dump trucks and cement type trucks, and these were very commonly seen on the road then, as well as now. The concept, so familiar in conversation of the sixties, was "built like a Mack truck." Well, that phrase did not come from a marginal product, it came from one that could take a lot of abuse, a product that went back to the war in Europe where Mack equipment dominated the landscape. Also such historical events as the building of the Hoover Dam where Mack mixers went around the clock providing the material to perform that massive undertaking. Other unusual divisions, Mack Fire, which at one time supplied all of New York City's fire trucks.

The Off-Highway Division was a product line of large trucks, mostly "end dumps," meaning that materials were dumped from behind. The size of these trucks made them exciting to me. Fifteen-ton loads. One hundred and twenty ton bottom dump. Prices on these ranged from eighty thousand dollars for a "little one" to three hundred thousand dollars for a monster. The tires alone were three to four thousand dollars each.

Well, when I met Harry (as Mr. Schaller wanted to be called) we discussed the possibility of me working for him. "My department is growing fast," he told me, "but I feel like I'm losing some control of it. What I need is a right hand man. Someone who's a self-starter, good with people. Someone who can make decisions on his own."

I thought—holy smoke, that person is me!

Then I told him so and he approved my raise in status and salary. The next thing I knew I had an office on the fifth floor. And as luck would have it, Harry's former secretary would now be acting as mine. Right from the start Harry let me do my thing, as he knew my intention was to improve our market share of off-highway vehicle sales and to reduce our operating cost. I wasted no time in contacting dealers and letting them know my desire was to create a winning situation for everyone. The only way to do that, I told them, was to find out our shortcomings and to create new programs that were virtually error-free. Although Mack had a price advantage as well as quality advantages in the overall market, we lost sales all the time to a competitor named Cat. They held the "lion's share" if you will, of the market, and there was less recognition of Mack because of them.

I started off by getting a lot done and by traveling cheaply and swiftly wherever I was needed, and putting in my usual overtime. I saved time, too, by not wasting any and I sent a loud instant message that we were in for a change, a change that would be aggressive in cutting costs at all levels.

Harry loved it. He sent me memos saying, "Good job!" And it's interesting how that little bit of recognition worked. Sometimes Harry dropped into my office wearing his characteristic black rim glasses, his full face smiling. He was holding one of my letters and halfway into my office he would say, "This got their attention!"

Lorraine Giovanni, our secretary enjoyed this as well because she too came from a middle class family where wastefulness was a sin.

Anyway, as a result of my example and encouragement, our dealers started to do a better job on stocking equipment. We placed more units on the line and in a short time there was a difference in sales. Most dealers were amazed that I would fly to some medium size town at the drop of a hat just to make a customer call. My intention was of course to present Mack as an alternative to Euclid or Cat. I had no problem jumping in a MACK 35-ton unit with a Detroit powered and an Allison tranny with a Heil or Atlas heated body that had exhaust roaring through it. I got under a 10-yard loader and waved the operator to load the baby up so we could see what a Mack could do.

The dealers had never experienced a real team player before. I went the extra mile for them by going to the factory with their concerns and they gave me the same cooperation in return. We attended huge shows such as at the McCormick in Chicago and we displayed our product with pride. One time we got Mario Andretti to sign autographs at a trade show. That really brought the crowds, too, and people saw what we were doing in a very favorable light.

My drive in doing demos and having the local salesperson on my call list got me some congratulatory letters from the new president of Mack. This was a man who started as a technician in Canada. His name was Mr. Pelletier and he seemed to be the very answer I was looking for—a self-made man who confirmed the idea that you could get to the top with hard work. As a natural-ized citizen I could not become president of the United States as our laws would not allow it; but I could become president of Mack Trucks.

I was now invited to eat at the executive cafeteria. (Actually cafeteria is a very bad word for describing this facility, which was better than most restaurants). At this upper-level environment, I got to eat and share stories with the top leaders in the firm. And it was music to my ears that the buzz around the tables was that Off Highway was the division to watch. One day Mr. Pelletier noticed me and questioned if I was that guy who had the head-to-head demo against a Euclid in one of the pits at Jasper, Alabama.

I replied that indeed I was the guy. In fact, I told him that contest had sealed the deal for Bill Wooten, a big dealer in Birmingham. Mr. Pelletier grinned and patted me on my left shoulder. "You have strong arms," he remarked.

"You should see my serve," I tossed back.

He asked, "Oh, do you play tennis?"

"Sure," I answered.

His smile returned. "We must play some day."

"Name the time, I'll be there."

Truthfully, I did not play tennis. I hardly knew the game but I had read that he did and I wanted to get some time with him. Therefore, in preparation, I went out and got a racket at the brand new Kmart store and I blew eight dollars on a strung racket and two cans of Penn balls for one dollar each. I practiced with my coach, Terry, a few times and got the basic rules and the one thing that was in my favor was the point is never over until it is over.

Then one day when I was not expecting it, Mr. Pelletier asked me to play tennis with him on Saturday. "Has to be in the morning," he said, "because I have to fly to Canada that afternoon." So we met at the club on Saturday. He was warming up and had all types of athletic elbow and knee supports. I asked myself if he was setting me up to feel sorry for him. Well, I had no intention of destroying him; I merely wanted to get to know him. "Warm up," he suggested. "We don't have to go at it so quickly."

So we volleyed for fifteen minutes after which he said, "OK, let's play."

To my surprise Mr. Pelletier was not a hard server, but just about every one went in. He could have me run from one corner to the other and back again. I now realized that this guy was really good and that I did not need to concern myself about exhausting him, but rather I needed to make sure I made a good showing.

He ran me ragged in short order, but I did not let him know it even though my throat was burning. I lost the first set to the old guy, 6 to 1. The second set I started with a winning game but ended up 6 to 2. I was worried about the third when he remarked, "It's getting late and I'm afraid I'll have to call it quits." I nodded and looked a little disappointed but inside I was saying, "Thank God." One of my best lessons in life. Mr. Pelletier was not young, nor was he very strong, but he whipped my ass and I was going to remember that experience is worth more than strength, and that knowing your opponent is everything. He knew me as soon as I started playing, and he went for my weakness.

That same game is played just that way every day of the world. In business, and in pleasure—know whom you are dealing with. In sales, particularly, I was going to concentrate on our competitor's weakness, and then exploit that to my own advantage.

Chapter Thirty-four

M ack was getting more exciting as I met with dealers and made sure that they did the proper demos. The experience I received was priceless. I visited mines where soft coal was being excavated by one hundred yard draglines that removed thirty to forty feet of overburden (land or dirt over the coal seam) and uncovering coal veins of thirty feet as well. You had loaders that cost over half a million dollar each loading a bunch of Macks 120-ton bottom dumps with coal. The bottom dumps would go over a bridge that had a long narrow opening in the center of it and the trucks would straddle that opening and unload their load to a long train of coal cars. This was the coal used to blow into furnaces that powered many power plants that generated electricity for various cities or mines smelting pots.

The dragline itself was this enormous piece of equipment that took numerous railroad cars of pieces to put together. It was powered by monstrous electrical motors and the power line itself to this piece of equipment had to be at least ten inches round.

Each time it would move dirt with a single bucket bite it would be moving 100-yard of material. Most people do not understand what a yard is or what a 100-yard is, other than it is 100 more. However, figure that each time it would be more material than eleven full Mack concrete trucks. The term the whole nine yards come from the fact that a basic concrete truck holds nine yards. So if someone wants an entire load they say the whole nine yards. Well this machine was moving eleven of these Mack loads each scoop.

I was in the hollows, as they say, in West Virginia and Kentucky about the places between two mountains. The type of coal in this area is hard coal and although it can be mined the same way, it is usually too costly as the vein is normally too far down and much too much dirt needs to be moved to get there. They use various techniques and one is to use a huge augur—a monster drill bit—that brings coal out as it digs in.

This type coal is much harder and much more valuable and of course more expensive to mine and certainly more dangerous for the workers.

On one of my trips I was visiting an underground mine not far from Grants, New Mexico, a few hours from Albuquerque. We had a very positive meeting with one of our Mack owners and the salesperson that I was with lending factory support to was so pleased with the help I was giving him, that he said, "On the way back to Albuquerque, let me show you where you can get some great souvenirs."

I told him, "You know, my wife asked me to check out some Indian jewelry."

"I've got a relative in Grants, who is in the business."

We pulled up at his relation's shop and I was amazed at the variety of the jewelry and also the subtle stylistic differences between the Navajo and Pueblo patterns. The Navajos were known for designs of leaves and ropes and things, while the Zunis seemed to do more complex inlaid stone work. This little shop had everything—sand paintings, bear claws, mother of pearl necklaces, beads, watch bands, bracelets and all kinds of rings, mostly with turquoise. I told the owner, "My plan is to take home a large variety of jewelry, including the mounted sand paintings, and if these are liked I am going to buy your stuff regularly by phone." I then bought as much as I could, which was about three hundred dollars worth.

When I got back to Wescosville, I could not wait to show the jewelry to Bette Ann. I spread it out on our coffee table—rings, bracelets, pendants, necklaces, bear claws, bolo ties. Bette Ann's eyes grew large. If I had covered the table in diamonds it would not have meant as much as this beautiful Indian jewelry from the Southwest.

She called several of her friends, and they came over to our house.

Soon they were asking, "How much is this? How much is that?"

Our next door neighbor, Lynn, asked me about one of the necklaces and I told her that that it was a signed piece. She said to Bette Ann, "Is it OK if I buy it?"

Bette Ann asked me if I could get more like it. I assured her that I could. I made a wooden display complete with mirrors and black velvet. The women spread the news that we were selling one-of-a-kind Indian jewelry. This got so popular that nurses used to call and come over after their shift to shop for items.

I was suddenly doing business where I had to buy five hundred dollars worth of jewelry at a time, and selling it as fast as I could set up my display. This went on for over a year and anytime that a piece, especially an expensive piece, would not move all I had to do was have my wife wear it once and it would sell.

At Mack things were going great. I had gotten a number of raises. Harry was very good to me, but no doubt I deserved it. Then I came up with the idea that our Southern region was an untapped gold mine, in that there was only one representative out of Knoxville. I felt that it should be divided. Another rep should be stationed out of Atlanta. When Harry asked who this might be, I grinned.

Well, Mack did not make quick decisions, but here was a good idea planted in my supervisor's head.

One day the executive vice president of marketing, Mr. Davis, asked me very bluntly about the opportunity in Atlanta. He said that he heard good things about me and not only from Harry but also from the dealers. "I hear you have some new ideas about improving our market share," he said. I told him, "Basically, we're just taking orders down there. What we need is someone who's hungry, someone who can make big improvements in that part of the country."

He furrowed his brow, as if trying to come up with someone.

"Who do you have in mind, Franco?"

"Someone like me," I said unabashedly.

He gave me a calculated smile. "You want to talk to your wife about this?"

I smiled back at him. "She's already on the same page with me. She knows my Bulldog goals as well as I do."

He laughed. "I think you better start packing then."

A little later, we agreed on salary and so forth. It turned out I was going to go backwards. I would not be making the thirty thousand dollars plus that I was then earning, but I would get one thousand dollars a month plus commission. And the commission part was a honey pot, as I saw it, because the Southern territory was wide open and unclaimed. I was going to open it up, and make a fortune. I was sure of it.

The following week the house went on the market and my neighbors were amazed when I told them what I was selling it for. But I forgot to mention that while I was selling jewelry, I was also getting my real estate license. Once I passed the test, I worked part time for a company in Wescosville that specialized in buying and selling "gentleman farms." Anyway, I was putting the house up for $56,900.00

The house sold quickly to a nice Italian lady for full price less appliance insurance. My next challenge was to go to Atlanta myself and check out the Mack Branch that I was about to make rich.

Georgia

Chapter Thirty-five

The dealership was on 780 Memorial Drive. Not a very nice place or facility, for that matter. The regional manager was John Baker and he was a proper suit kind of guy with distinguished white hair and he used a decorative cane when he walked. From what I had heard through the grapevine, Mr. Baker was not thrilled to have a Yankee and especially an "I-talian" shoved down his throat. However, as much as he did not like it, he also did not have the balls to say anything to the big boys at world headquarters other than to ask if they thought I would be able to fit in. Once they responded "You're damn right Franco will fit in, he can fit anywhere!" Baker chuckled as I learned he would do under nervous conditions.

I met a bunch of the people there and they were all very nice. Some I had met in the past in my travels through Atlanta. Others in Mack meetings, and still others knew me through the Mack publications that I was in. I was advised to move to the east part of Atlanta where there were new subdivisions going up, nice schools, and the drive to work was not that bad.

Dekalb County was huge. Atlanta was a big city. One thing I noticed was that the area around the dealership was depressing. It was very run down and almost a wino area, but once you got into the actual city of Atlanta it was beautiful and amazingly clean. Our realtor was very southern, and I loved the way she talked. Her name was Bette Rose. I told her "You'd get along with my wife Bette Ann." She chuckled, "Are you from New York?"

Even today I get that question and I usually reply that I entered through New York but my home has been all of America.

Anyway I narrowed my house hunting to Stone Mountain, Georgia.

Two of the district managers lived in Stone Mountain; Chuck Gehrmann lived right behind the mountain and Paul Cantrell lived in front of it. Well, the front of the Mountain had huge homes and out of our league (at the moment) so we decided to look at the back area. We found a subdivision with lots of trees. Bette Rose told me "In Atlanta we get a number of ice storms and pine trees do not do so well, so if we can we should find a lot or home with hardwood trees."

As luck would have it we found a large hardwood lot, one acre plus, with a tri-level home, four bedrooms and two baths. There was a two-car garage, and a southern-looking front porch. The construction was fieldstone and cedar and the front windows were very tall and narrow and cranked open. The home had so many nice things, but mostly it was a cheerful home with a view of the beautiful woods at every window.

I told Bette Rose, "I like it and I am sure that my wife will like it as well." The house was listed at $69,500.00. I offered $65,900.00, which was the most I could afford.

I flew Bette Ann down and we drove right to Stone Mountain. It was kind of late so Bette Ann's impression in the darkness kind of scared her. We stayed at the Stone Mountain Inn, an ante-bellum style hotel in the middle of a park with waitresses dressed as they did one hundred years ago. From our hotel window you could see the famous carving on the mountain of famous southern heroes on their horses. It was breath-taking at dusk. Both of us were excited, but Bette Ann was still a little undecided. In the morning The Raven Springs Subdivision looked a lot more friendly.

We finalized the paperwork that day, flew home, and began our trip south. When we left Wescosville on our way to Stone Mountain, Amie was eight and Buddy was four. We followed each other on the highway and I had the dog and Bette Ann had both children for the first half of the trip. Buddy got sick and I took him with me and we arrived in Georgia late the same day. I stopped at the Mack dealership so that I could introduce my family. Following the visit I drove along Memorial drive that looked like a war zone. To Bette Ann's surprise, I turned into a driveway that led to a blue shack. I got out of the car. Bette Ann, looking worried, followed me.

I walked up to her car and looked at Amie (I can still see her huddling next to her Mom) I said, "Well here we are—home!" Amie took a look both ways hoping there was something she had missed. Then she said, "No way Dad!" I laughed and told Bette Ann to back out. When we got to 601 Raven Springs, the kids went nuts. They loved the land, the trees, and the house. And I think after the blue shack experience, the new home looked great.

I began a real friendship with my associate, Chuck. There was no competition between us and we often traveled together or arranged to meet in the same town. We had a lot in common. Chuck was five or six years older and he was raised in Pittsburgh area where most of his friends were Italian (not I-talian). He also had a daughter and a son. We both felt same about Mr. Baker.

So now I visited various regional dealers, and having worked with them in various capacities in the past, it did not take long for me to get to know them well and we started working on programs that benefited everyone. Work went smoothly. At home I built a bar in the recreation room downstairs. I ripped a hole in the wall, added French doors and a spacious deck. I used cedar to give it that aged look, and also to match the rest of the house.

I then built a tree house for Amie and her new friends. This tree house was not a normal one of course, but an Antonetti hand-crafted home in miniature. I got scrap lumber from the developer who became a friend right away. Anyway the tree house had a real roof, windows, and I built it entirely out of cedar. It was at least fifteen feet high and the stairs leading up were very sturdy.

One of my inside projects was to line the entire wall going upstairs with cedar up to about thirty six inches to make it look good and also to reduce the cleaning of walls from Buddy's hands. The other cute project was in our laundry closet upstairs. I cut a neat hole at the bottom of it and made a laundry chute with leftover duct material. After that it was a breeze to throw our laundry down the chute, and it ended up in a basket right next to the washing machine.

One day Buddy decided to go down the chute himself, but he quickly got stuck.

Bette Ann panicked, called the fire squad, and they were pretty cool about it. They had to dismantle the lower duct to finally get him out, and once that was done she had to beg them to put it back together,

I became friendly with sales rep Jim Judy at Cralle Hall Mack one of our dealerships in Tampa. He took me to some local cigar factories where cigars were still handmade. I observed how each cigar was rolled, how each case of cigars had to have the color of the outside leaves. If this match was imperfect, the cigars were taken out and placed into the seconds category. Well, that aroma and education got me into cigar smoking and I bought the second cases. At that time a good cigar (not a great cigar) would cost about two to three dollars each. A case that held thirty cigars sold for forty to fifty dollars. I liked the medium cigars as they smelled and tasted good, and I could afford to smoke four to five a day, My brand would go retail for thirty to forty dollars for top of the line but my seconds ran about fifteen dollars a case.

In Atlanta I began to like grits. The first time I saw them they looked and tasted like wall paste. Finally, I learned to use butter and salt, and then they were delicious. I also liked biscuits and gravy, collard greens, and my favorite was crackling corn bread. Next to the Atlanta prison there was this hole-in-the-wall restaurant that was always packed. They were famous for Brunswick stew and crackling corn bread.

By now things were going so well, I joined a country club and started to play tennis. The kids enjoyed the swimming pool there, too.

Chuck loved motorcycles. He used to race bikes and he actually made a living at it. Chuck was a wiry little devil who could eat all day, and never gain a pound. Well, one day Chuck told me that he had joined up with one of this other Italian friends and together they had purchased a Yamaha dealership in Stone Mountain. I was excited for him. I said, "Maybe I should be your first customer."

He said, "What is it you want?"

I shrugged. "I don't have a motorcycle license and I have no idea what I should buy."

Chuck grinned. "I'll take care of the license. What color do you prefer?"

I said, "I want a black bike with gold trim."

"No problem,"

Chuck was famous for his two-minute teases. He would come up one day with a Porsche that he had just bought or a Ferrari that he borrowed. We loved cars and we drove each other crazy always talking about the cars we saw or rented at various places. Anyway, one morning Chuck came in as we were all having breakfast, and he said, "I got your bike!"

"No kidding!" We went outside. In front of the garage there was a big wooden crate.

"Is the bike in there?" I asked.

"Yeah," Chuck said. "Get some tools."

So as we opened layers of brown paper and down deep were the bike parts. I noticed that the bike was bright red, not black. I said, "Chuck it's red!"

He said, " Yeah, red, black—close enough!"

I shrugged. He was my buddy. What was the difference? It was just a color.

So, we put the bike together and, of course I got my license and we had a ball with this new Yamaha X S 400.

At this point in my life everything was going smoothly. The children were going to school; Amie was at the local public school and Buddy had gone to Rocking Home Ranch pre-school. This was a good environment for kids, as our subdivision was made up of professional people, hard workers who were trying to provide their family with the finer things in life.

The only thing different in my life was this: Not only was I only working for commissions but for the first time I had no part-time jobs. My expenses were growing but not my income. However, I had opened up two dealerships to larger sales—these were in South Florida and in Tampa. Things began to pick up.

Meanwhile I loved living in Stone Mountain. Our jail was a converted train station. The town drunk occasionally got locked up so he would not hurt himself, but other than that the place was just decorative. The local pharmacy had a soda fountain area where you could get authentic malt and a sugar coated ice cream cone for a quarter. The old post office was now a buffet restaurant. Good friends of Chuck who later became friends of ours, took on this high risk that became an instant success. On the way home from the center of town which was less than two miles away, there was a local store called *Buddy's*. All in all, we felt right at home.

Chapter Thirty-six

I decided to become a Mason, as Fred was a Mason, and every so
often he told me the good things that Masons did, and especially the Shriners. You cannot become a Shriner until you are a
Mason, as masonry is the foundation of these other fraternities
and one of the rules is that you are not permitted to seek entry
into the organization. However, once you are asked and you have a
willing sponsor, he petitions that particular lodge, and the process
begins. I found out that Chuck was a Mason but not in good
standing, for one reason or another. Mostly because he moved a
lot and never got his dues paid or transferred. I inquired around
and found a guy in Stone Mountain Lodge 449 who told me how
much work it was to be a member. He said there was also a lot to
memorize too. And he questioned the fact that I was Catholic.

"What's wrong with that?" I wanted to know.

"Well, we'll accept a Catholic or a Jew, for that matter, but I
wonder if the Catholic Church will allow you to join an organization
that has some secrecy to it."

I told him, "I have no problem with any of this. Neither the
dedication nor the time, nor the stuff that has to be learned. As
for the Church, what do they know about Franco or Stone
Mountain?"

I must say that it was not easy. I was on the road a great deal
and there was a lot of studying to do for the membership. With my
travels it made it that much more difficult, but I truly enjoyed the
work. Bette Ann put up with Masonic teachers who were over at
the house whenever I was home.

Our lodge, believe it or not, was on property owned by the
KKK. I questioned this and learned about Stone Mountain and
the cross burning days of long ago. Fortunately, the people in
lodge 449 were no part of that. Most were old good old boys

who used to call me kid as I was one of the youngest at thirty-four. So, I became a Mason and I was proud of it. Fred was beside himself with joy. He wished that Freddy had followed in his footsteps, but Freddy chose not to.

Now, my next step was to become a Shriner. I eventually got my 32 degrees and became a Shriner out of the Yaarab Temple in Atlanta, Georgia. There is another degree available to a Shriner and that is the 33rd degree. That degree, however, is not one that you can study for. It is a degree that is given to you by others, and it is earned by doing something that is out of the ordinary. A number of our presidents were Shriners and they also had the honor of being 33rd degree Shriners. As I write I still am a Mason and Shriner in good standing.

One of our elder Masons had a heart attack one day, and having found out about it I visited him and his wife. He was in pretty bad shape, but he was also one of the individuals who helped raise me (a term used when becoming a Mason) and the best I could do was visit him and try to boost him up some. He was glad to see me, but the second time I visited him I brought over a gallon of red Italian wine.

I had told him that when Grandpa had a heart attack, the doctor said that a small glass of red wine every day would be good for him. Well, this gentleman did not drink. However, at my next visit, his wife was eager to tell me that he did try a little wine. She said it relaxed him and he liked it.

He confirmed this when he told me, "Hey! Franco! That guinea red is great!"

One day I saw a go-cart for sale by the side of the road. This was one of those with a fiberglass body, and oversize air tires. It looked like a blue dune buggy. Later I found out that it had been used for Shriner parades, and had all the necessary suspension modification and souped-up engine. They wanted four hundred dollars. Seemed like a lot, but being an impulsive buyer I offered three hundred and fifty, take it or leave it, and they took it.

Once at the house, the kids went nuts and Bette Ann made a silly look with her eyebrows, not a mad way, but amused. We had a little go-cart for Buddy that we brought down from Pennsylvania—now this monster. I got into it myself and with that 5-horse power engine, push button start, and special centrifugal clutch, watch out. I started it and with a loud powerful sound she came alive.

Amie was a tough cookie; she could do anything her Dad could do. She knew how to handle go-carts. Buddy was pretty good with the little one but I was not about to let him try this monster. Well, we allowed Mommy to try it first. She took off up the street up to the clubhouse and all her friends saw her. I could hear when she floored it and backed off, as the exhaust noise was loud. Then it was Amie's turn. I warned her drive it very slow. We were on a dead-end street and I wanted her to get used to it.

"Yes Daddy. Yes Daddy. I know Daddy. OK Daddy." She was very eager to go.

So she went down our driveway nice and easy, pressing the disc brakes as she proceeded to go around the street. She disappeared from view. Then, all at once I heard the engine open up full throttle. She roared past the clubhouse and did a turn around near our friends the Norberrys and then she began flying down the hill. Just before she came around the corner, she slowed to a crawl.

I looked at Bette Ann, and said "What a pisser your daughter is!"

I also got a huge trampoline with a fourteen foot circumference. I was pretty good at flips so it was easy for me to teach Buddy. For some reason, though, I could do a backward flip like nothing but the forward flip was more difficult. I showed Buddy how to do it, and then I held his back and I flipped him. He loved it. Amie on the other hand rushed into everything, all guts and glory, and she got hurt more often than Buddy did.

I bought some anchor rope—the kind you use to anchor a yacht. I got it for a song at a garage sale. I climbed one of our hardwood trees in the back yard, and at about fifteen feet I secured the rope, and made a rubber tire swing. I now took the other end of the rope that I had just tied at the other tree and climbed at a tree at least twenty feet away and as the backyard was laid out nothing would be in the way.

Next I took a tire and tied it off at about two feet off the ground—and now I had an enormous swing. I tried it first and asked Amie to give me a shove while Bette Ann and Buddy watched. I started swinging on my own after Amie had given me a few shoves. Bette Ann saw me swinging on it, flying high as I could, and she said, "Who is the real kid, you or the children?"

Amie was next up. I pushed her so hard and got her going about twenty feet off the ground. She was speechless with pleasure. Then it was Buddy's turn, and of course he ate it up. He was a little devil and he loved scary things, and this was plenty scary without being really dangerous.

I had a formula in my mind that came from no specific study; it was just my way of measuring success. The way I saw it, you should make at least one thousand dollars for each year of your age. I had been ahead of my formula when I left Allentown, but when we first moved to Georgia I fell below my formula. That was scary as I had to dip into my savings and my savings were never much as we always lived on the edge. This year however, I actually came close to doubling my average, which was not bad for a 34 year- old with no college education.

I was in Charlotte, North Carolina one day and found out that one of our customers was coming off a lease on a gorgeous 1978 Seville. It was light blue with a white vinyl top with opera lights. It was so clean that one could smell the fragrance of "new car" all over it. I decided to buy it on the spot and I had it sent to our branch in Atlanta. I asked Bette Ann to have lunch with me the day it arrived and I told her the car was hers. Well, after the "You are kidding? Really? Come on! For sure? OK whose is it really? And I LOVE YOU," she said, "Let me drive it."

I ended up giving away our wagon to one of the mechanics, who was having a hard time. In reality that car was free and clear and no big deal, so I was glad to help someone out.

Now our accountant said one day in his good o boy drawl, "Hey boy you need to do something."

I said, "What would you like me to do?"

He replied, "Buy something. Get a rental home."

I gave that some thought. A few miles from our home in Stone Mountain there was a cute starter home for about thirty thousand dollars and I bought it. I had it rented out before it was completed and I got four hundred and forty dollars a month income on it.

Chuck and I both were on top of the world at this time. Mr. Baker was pretty happy too. He had expected problems from me when I came down as I was another northerner, and Chuck was no different, just older and a little less wild. The fact that we were exceeding our quotas and that the dealers liked us and that as a result Mr. Baker was making additional bonuses did not hurt our relationship.

Another thing that made Atlanta a great location for us was that Freddy was stationed in Panama City and he had purchased a condo right on the water. We would at times take off after work and if all was well we could make it there in six hard hours. The kids had the Miracle Mile to cruise with their family and the sand dunes, as well as diving for sand dollars. We all had a very good happy life to this point. I made sure that they never experienced the tough times I had been through. When I think of all the times

I kissed Amie or Buddy on the lips and the thousands of hugs we shared, it all seemed perfectly natural. But when I tried to think of a single time that one of my parents kissed me, I could not do it. Such is life.

I had the opportunity to find a home being listed near the rental home I had and it was a three bedroom as well and I made an offer that I did not expect to be accepted, but it was. So now I had two rentals. The second rental brought in another four hundred dollars a month.

Chapter Thirty-seven

Bad news came when I was told that Grandpa had passed away. I flew back and assisted in making the final arrangements. We had mass at The Little Flower Church, where we got married. We buried Grandpa in Summit and I do not know why it happens, but so many times at funerals, it rains cats and dogs. This was one of those times.

Now my mother and grandmother were all alone in the house on Garfield Street.

I attempted to get my mother out of there, but after so many years it was hopeless, and I knew she would be there until Suzy died. Tough as my mother was, Suzy was tougher, and at eighty-four she was tougher than ever. I saw my brother at the funeral and he told me that the parts division of Mack was moving to Maryland, and he was not about to go there. I told him that prior to working at Mack he did not have a nice house or the benefits he was enjoying. "But if you don't want to move, don't!" I told him.

He said, "I took a vacation to Vegas not long ago and when I was there my wrist, you know the one I broke years ago, stopped hurting. Vegas seems like a good place to live."

I asked, "What about work?"

"I can get by working for a cleaners. I still know how to press clothes, and I hear that there's a lot of work in Vegas like that."

I had lost interest in my brother long ago so I told him, "Whatever works for you is what you should do, but I think that leaving Mack is crazy." A few months later, he did indeed go to Vegas. I was amazed, as he was not a person to make decisions, especially big ones.

My mother also handed me a bunch of letters that had come from Italy from an attorney. They basically said that my father wanted a divorce; new laws had been passed and divorce was now permitted. My mother was livid. "How can that bastard want a divorce now after twenty-five years in this country and us separated since you were one year old?"

I figured that I would write back to the attorney since I was the only one who could read and write Italian. I wanted to let him know that he had not provided my mother with child support since I was born. To my surprise the attorney wrote back two months later saying that they were proceeding with the divorce. As for child support, the lawyer explained that Mr. Pasquale Antonetti had four children not five. It was a hell of a way to confirm my belief but a load came off my shoulders when I read that statement. I decided that when I called my mother that I would keep this news to myself, as it served no purpose to let her know.

Chuck and I were having some good months at work. The Off Highway Department had struck a deal for twenty trucks and we were in tall cotton, as they say. Now we were gearing up for our yearly meeting at the Moscone Center in the Bay area.

Every dealer attended this along with his or her sales force. This was the time to get pumped up about the new product lines. In my case, I knew that I was going to get at least one or more awards. My numbers were outstanding. I was excited to spend this time in the Bay area at Fisherman's Wharf with my best friends—how great was that? The day finally came and Chuck and I left the women—Bette Ann at my house and Joan at his— and off we went to Hartfield airport which was one of the most modern and yet also one of the easiest airports to fly out of, so we went to San Francisco without a care. We arrived in time to see a few sights before calling it a night at the historic and beautiful Saint Francis Hotel. I called Bette Ann just before I turned the lights off, and let her know that all was well, and that I would give her the good news tomorrow night.

The following morning we all had breakfast, and everyone was chipper. We were ready for a lot of new stuff and hoped that we would not have to listen to a lot of dry speeches. Basically, we wanted to see the new products that would kick ass next year. And especially important, who won what award. Some dealers would get four hundred unit sales plaques, which is a whole lot of trucks. We had dealers from Puerto Rico, Canada, and all kinds of people from our International Department.

Many of our dealers won in our region. It felt good to see an individual you knew who had worked extra hard or made some sacrifices to get the recognition he or she deserved. At this time my heart was beating fast. I was more concerned how I might be introduced. Also I did not want to come across as cocky. I wanted to be appreciative, yet deserving. Award after award and nothing about our division. Finally, it was the closing ceremony, and we were about to be excused. I was baffled, to say the very least. I looked at about eight rows behind me, and across the aisle I could see Harry my old boss, who ran the division. He did not look good either. What was going on? As soon as we were dismissed, I crawled over a bunch of people and grabbed Harry's jacket.

"Harry what the hell happened?"

With his index finger over his nose he motioned that I should follow him. We had to wait for a while. A million people seemed to be going by, and the noise was deafening. Finally Harry spoke with a soft voice and real tears.

"I could not tell you before," he said, "but the Off Highway Department is out of business. We are finished!"

"What do you mean? Our business is way up."

"Yes, your business is up. But the other regions are way down. You see, the coal business has dried up, and Mack needs to put their money where they get the best return."

I felt as if I was falling into a deep hole.

"Am I out of a job?"

Harry's face was gray and tired. "We're all out of a job," he said.

"You got to be kidding," I told him.

He shook his head solemnly.

"I expected an award, not a kick in the ass." Harry shook his head, and patted me on the back. That was my award.

It was a stupid thing to do but I called Bette Ann, and cried my eyes out while I told her that the company closed down our division, and I had no idea what was going to happen to us. Surprisingly, she was much better at accepting this blow than I was. She responded by telling me how great I was, and that people would fight for me because I was the best salesperson anybody had ever seen.

"Don't worry, go find Chuck and have a good time."

I met up with Chuck and a few other guys, and we went out for a few drinks and a good cigar. I don't drink more than a Rusty Nail with dinner. Maybe a second one, but that was my usual limit. I do not know how many Chuck bought me that night but it did not make me sick. I was not feeling any pain and fortunately I was not driving, as there was a trolley that dropped us off right in front of the hotel. I slept like a baby and in the morning Dick Murphy approached me and said that he was starting a new division of trucks. He said it was a joint venture with Renault.

"Mack and Renault have been working for a long time on the mid-range truck made in France with a Mack engine modified to European specs with a turbo and an after-cooler and many other American components. These trucks are available in this country, but they're not meant for long hauls." Mr. Murphy gave me a serious look.

"You interested?" he asked.

I wanted to say, "Does a bear shit in the woods?" But instead I nodded several times and said yes.

Flying home was a little easier knowing that I had the possibility of a new job even though I did not know where, or for how much or any other thing. At least it was a possibility.

When I to returned Atlanta I was asked to go to Allentown to interview for the new position in selling the new Mid-Liner truck. The new job with Mr. Murphy happened quickly. I was one of the lucky few. I dove into the product, asked to drive it, and spent as much time around it as they would allow me at the proving grounds at back in Allentown.

My previous hands-on experience with many of the dealers, as well as my reputation as a salesperson, helped me become—almost overnight—the most successful Mid-Liner representative in the company. We had six representatives assigned to the U.S. and I went at it with my usual passion and commitment.

At my first major presentation in Miami I said, "I understand that you guys are concerned about taking on a new line especially one you know nothing about or certainly very little about. I was put in the exact situation as you guys a few months ago when I had to make a decision that affected my family and financial future in leaving the Off Highway division and joining the Mid-Liner. I went to a lot of trouble to learn the product before a decision was made. I ask all of you or at least some of you, to please follow me to the parking lot downstairs for a five to ten minute show-and-tell and if you do not like what you see or what I have to say, I promise not another peep out of me the rest of the meeting."

I had arranged with the bellhops to park these two chassis (no bodies) next to each other. One was the 200 series and the other the 300 series, I rattled off all the American components like the Cuttler tanks, the Eaton two speed 18,500 rears, the Spicer drive shafts, the interchangeable wheels. I went on about the axles—the new spring package with the heavy axle in the rear. And I basically went crazy over the Mack engine that was an inline six cylinder that was not thrown away, but an engine designed with not only a turbo but an after cooler like your finer Volvo cars have and designed to drive at sixty miles an hour or more for an extended period of time, and finally, in the middle of me catching my breath, the dealer said, "OK you made your point."

That same day we sold over one hundred units to Ryder and our V.P. was astonished and he gave me credit for turning the whole show my way. I kept at it, too. I took salespeople outside and encouraged them to touch and feel the unit and some I took for a ride which was as comfortable as some cars.

Our office manager of the branch on Memorial Drive came to me one day as he knew I liked cars and let me know that at Decatur (near Atlanta) he saw this beautiful Mercedes convertible for sale. I went to check it out and it was a 1979 Mercedes 450 SL; it was light blue with European lights, two tops. It was less than a year old and they wanted $32,000.00. My Eldorado was getting old and Bette Ann's Seville was a great car that she used sparingly. I liked it a lot so I figured that I might get her this car and I would give one of the techs my car at $2,000.00. Then the SL would cost me about $30,000.00.

I got the car for $30,000.00 so now I owed $28,000.00 but things were still good.

I asked my Bette Ann to go with me to our Italian store so we could buy pumpkin seeds. She agreed and early on a Saturday morning we were on our way. She noticed right away that we were taking a different route but we would do that at times, as we enjoyed the fresh air and liked to see different parts of the Atlanta area. Sometimes we would go to Peach Tree Plaza to the famous round hotel just for a salad and a drink. So she expected a fun sightseeing ride before my stop at the Italian market.

As I got to Decatur I slowed down by the car dealer and there was the car—sparkling in the sun. It was part of the deal to detail it beautifully and have it filled and parked outside by 11:00 AM. I pulled next to it and told Bette Ann that someday I would like to see you in a car like that. She responded that we have too many things to worry about at this time and that Mercedes are for rich people and are a stupid investment. I told her that I wanted to look at it, as Chuck could be interested. Now she was concerned that the owner or salespeople would think that we are a couple of jerks, as we were dressed very casually.

I finally said, "Why don't you follow me home with your new car?"

"I know you are kidding. We can't afford this."

"You're right we can't afford it. But we bought it—so let's go!"

I can still see her now with her very curly blond hair blowing in the wind, and how she had to stop at Majic Market to get bread that we already had. And how excited she was talking about the car to Edie Norburry, one of her best friends.

I felt this was a small reward for her giving me such good advice the night I lost my old job in San Francisco.

Chapter Thirty-eight

One evening before I left home on a business trip, I made my normal rounds to make sure all was well around the house. Our back patio porch light was out. I got a replacement bulb and stepped out the back door with my right foot. It was totally dark out there. I felt an agonizing sharp pain. Somehow I knew at once what had happened. And, although I had never been bitten by a poisonous snake, I knew that that is what had happened to me. I was now in agony and I did exactly the wrong thing. I kept going from the back yard to the front, as if some strange momentum was carrying me along. The truth was, I was both scared and hurt. Finally, I knocked hard at the front door scaring Amie who was downstairs watching television. Bette Ann let me in and I was yelling that I had been bitten and still had not seen the thing that bit me—but I knew it was a snake. Amie yelled as she saw the snake slide into the house through the door that I had left open in the back. Buddy appeared with Amie as the serpent slid across the floor towards them. For a moment, I was frozen, not knowing what to do. Then Bette Ann picked up a monkey wrench that I had left on the bar a few hours earlier and she struck the head of the reptile and with one blow killed it.

The pain was rising up my inner thigh towards my groin. Amie said "Dad, it's a diamondback rattler!"

I refused to believe that, replying, "No it's not!"

Bette Ann asked, "What should we do now?"

I said, "Let me rest."

"No way, we are going the hospital right now." Then she grabbed a dustpan and pushed the writhing, but dead snake into it. The drive to the hospital was eerie—me, in such agony that I thought, "Maybe this is it, the one time I do not get away from the Grim Reaper.

Bette Ann drove out of our dark subdivision. She passed Majic Market and the Buddy Store and on to Memorial Drive. She crossed Memorial Drive which was like crossing a freeway. Time passed very slowly. We entered the Emergency Room at the hospital, but when a nurse saw Bette Ann's dust pan, she let us go first. I was putting all of my weight on my left leg, protecting my right bitten ankle.

We were escorted to a small room for the doctor in attendance. It had now been forty minutes since I was bitten.

At last an old doctor came in, walking and talking very slow. He instructed me to sit on the table.

"My daughter said that this snake is a diamond back rattler, is that true?" showing the doctor the contents of her dustpan.

The doctor's lower lip angled off to one side, and he said, "Naw, that's no diamondback, that's a copperhead!"

I asked, "It's not poisonous, is it?"

Long ago my mother had said I could not die, well, I wondered—what now?

Two nurses came in and asked if they could "borrow" the snake. It was all over the hospital that someone had gotten bitten by a poisonous snake and they were going to get it and play tricks on the staff. Good for them. But I was in agony.

Now the good old doctor got a needle that looked like a pole vault. He proceeded to harpoon me with it just below the bite. That hurt like hell.

"Well, that's that," I said with a painful sigh.

"Naw," he said, "I got to do it at each end, so get ready for three more hits."

You have absolutely no idea about how I much I dislike needles. But I survived the harpooning, by then the discoloration from my ankle was ugly and there were mean red streaks running up my leg toward my groin. I asked the doctor if I could go home now.

Without any hesitation he said "Naw."

"If the shots are working I should be able to go home."

"Naw," he replied. Then he told me he was concerned about my heart.

"What do you mean my heart?"

"It could fur-bo-late."

And just as he said it, I felt a fur-bo-la-tion.

Then he slowly explained that the heart could start beating so fast that you can die from it if you are not under the immediate care of a physician.

Let me tell you after hearing that I did not wiggle my eyelashes. I was so scared I stopped doing anything except breathing. I just sat still, and stared at the wall. After a few hours, the doctor said it was all right to leave, and we did.

The copperhead was placed in a large glass jar filled with formaldehyde.

I missed three days of work—a first, for me. But my mother's prophecy proved true again. I was alive. And I had a new word to use on the kids. "Naw."

Chapter Thirty-nine

Bette Ann and the kids got me a big surprise that I did not need at this time. This was a husky with bright blue eyes. Although a puppy, it was quite big already.

"We already have a dog," I said.

"Fanny is great and we love her but she is not a real dog," Amie said.

"What are you talking about?" I said.

"Well, she's more like a person," Buddy put in.

I could see that Buddy wanted more than anyone, a dog that he could rough up and play with. Fanny was maybe a little too delicate for him.

Anyway, I gave in pretty quickly and we named the newcomer Duchess. So, now I had to worry about a dog. So did Fanny. She was not a happy camper. But in the end they became friends.

While I was healing, Duchess took off a number of times, and the tears from Buddy were endless as I drove up and down the streets and walked the woods until I finally found her. My concern was that she might get run over. I decided to make a long dog run in the back of the house, and some of the run would actually go to the woods underneath the tree house. It all worked out except the "eye" on the cable kept wearing out. Well, the run was eighty feet long and the dog gave that eyelet a good workout. I tried washers and metal rings, but in no time they wore down to nothing.

One day at work I was talking to our parts manager about Duchess and he showed me some huge bearings off of a Mack wheel. He was about to discard them.

"One of these weighs three pounds, there's no way she could wear it out." he said.

I said, "Who cares what it weighs as long as it does the job."

So that night I took the wire down and inserted this monster race through it and reattached the wire and made it real tight. With the chain hooked up to it, we gave Duchess and the race a good test. She took off and the race would follow and when she stopped it took awhile for the race to stop and sometimes pulled her a few feet. But generally it was a success. However when Buddy came from school the next day, he went to give Duchess a hug. When she came to him at a gallop, she stopped abruptly as she usually did but the race kept on going, cracking Buddy on the head. Let me tell you, he was a bloody mess. I came home after getting a panic call, and found Bette Ann with Buddy with his head under the tap. He had quite a gash on his head. Bette Ann wanted me to take him to the hospital, but one of our family jokes is that "Dad can fix anything with a butterfly." So, I shaved him a little and he was calm, as both our kids have had their share of bangs and bruises. That is part of growing up and letting them be kids. I took some good size band-aids and made the appropriate butterflies for this wound. He was OK and after I got finished with him, I corrected the race by raising the wire another foot.

The kids did some nice growing up in Stone Mountain as we took train rides around the mountain. We traveled to Ashville to see the Biltmore house, and Look Out Mountain in Chattanooga, visited Savannah, and also saw some of the beautiful old oaks covered with Spanish moss in Charleston, South Carolina.

At bedtime Bette Ann told the kids the normal bedtime story that any other healthy kid in America would be told. When my turn came, Buddy usually asked for a specific story. I would not tell him that story because, first of all, I never heard of this Humpty Dumpty stuff or Jill and some guy running up the hill. So I made up these tear-jerking tales like "Johnny and the Bluebird." I just made it up as I went along and it would be about a kid finding a hurt bird and him saving it and so on. The next time it came for a story I invented another—"Mickey and the

Race Bike." It was easier for me to come up with a brand new one than trying to remember the old made-up one.

I found out years later that when Buddy was in school he always asked the teacher if she had the book, "Johnny and the Bluebird" or about "Mickey and the Race Bike". Of course the teacher had not seen these books, as I had not written them yet. Maybe one day....

Those are some things that made growing up with Dad a little different. As far as my own family, however, I had not communicated with anyone in Italy to this point. It had been over twenty-five years since I left Italy. In the time I knew for sure that my dad was not my Dad, I tried phoning my Uncle Orazio but his wife would never let me speak to him. That saddened me but one day I found out that the middle sister Maria (Ofelia) was going to visit my mother, my mother was paying for the fare from Rome to Newark, New Jersey.

She would stay with my mother for thirty days so there was no need of special paperwork for this visit. How timely is that, I thought. I contacted my mother and told her that I would like to see my sister and if she would allow me, I would fly her to Atlanta. My mother moaned that she did not have enough time to let Ofelia come to Atlanta. Finally after my sister arrived she asked about me and wanted to visit, so my mother gave in. Our meeting at the airport was strange. What I saw before me did not look like Ofelia. But more like my skinny older sister. Of course, what had happened was that Ofelia had just lost a lot of weight. Anyway, we talked forever. The kids did not want to go to bed. They listened to every word we said: Maybe they could not understand the language but they could see the gestures and figure it out.

After a few days we decided to take her to Disney World. She had not been in such a nice car as Bette Ann's but it was too crowded to take the Mercedes so we took the Seville and that was tight enough for the four hundred and seventy-two mile drive one way. (Thank God, our neighbors were nice enough to take care of our dogs.)

We stayed at the Contemporary. At that time that was the best hotel around. Ofelia marveled at the tram going through the hotel and the room with the balcony allowing us to see the fireworks each night. One night we took her to see the parade.

Translating was not difficult, just tiresome, as I was going back and forth telling her what my kids said, and then explaining to them what she said. At one point I started to talk in English to my sister and Italian to Bette Ann. During this four-day stay we purchased additional luggage to hold the clothing and gifts we were buying for Ofelia.

In her mind, I guess, we were rich Americans. The parade started and Ofelia was talking a mile a minute. I saw a tiny tear in the corner of her eye. I asked her what she was feeling and she told me that she felt like an anchovy. It made absolutely no sense to me but I had left Italy long ago, and my Italian was limited so I just shrugged.

Bette Ann asked, "What did Ofelia say?"

I said, "She said she feels like an anchovy." Bette Ann looked surprised. At that point, we let it go and continued to watch the parade. Then, once my sister started to say the Italian word for anchovy, *alice*, it suddenly made sense. She was trying to say she felt like Alice in Wonderland. We had a great time and I got her back to my mother's and, hopefully, she told that funny story to my sisters.

Chapter Forty

One morning Bette Ann and I were having breakfast in front of the large bay window that faced the woods. We were admiring how nice the kids were playing. Amie was on the trampoline. She had mastered the easy flip—she jumped a few times and then fell to her knees and on the way back up flipped forward with a quick easy motion.

Buddy, on the other hand, was doing flips like a wild man but at this particular moment he found an actual live vine that dangled from one of our trees and was giving it a few test pulls and a little ride as well. As we watched him you could see his smile grow as he increased his height with the swing. Each time he glided back he would kick off the ground with a little more force, and soon he was flying. He was now going so high that it appeared that he was going to come through our window. I motioned to him with my right hand telling him to back off as he was going too high. You could tell by his wide-open mouth and his bright shiny teeth that he was not about to slow down. Just then the vine broke in the midst of an upward window glide, and what appeared to be a slow motion fall—Buddy flying through the air with only a portion of the vine still in his hands, and heading for us feet first. He fell short of the window but managed to crack his head on our concrete sitting benches. We had blood, all right, and not far behind the blood, a new butterfly. We still have the table and benches today and they have traveled thousands of miles in all the various moves, but they are too precious to get rid of.

One day we tried to sell one of the local companies a Mid-Liner for their pecan factory. In the process we learned a great deal about pecans. One of the cool things about sales is that you can learn so much from others about what they do. The Stone Mountain Pecan Factory specialized in processing pecans that came from the pecan capitol of the world, Albany, Georgia. The trees are actually shaken by a very powerful machine and once the nuts fall to the ground, their machine picks them up. The pecan pick-up cart looks just like the ones you see at a driving range picking up golf balls.

Anyway, the nuts are shipped to various wholesalers or factories like the one in Stone Mountain. The nuts go through a huge wash bin and afterwards a large tumbler similar to the round tube that we used to walk through at amusement parks. The only difference was that this tumbler was closed at both ends. The final operation was extremely labor intensive; the broken nuts traveled on a conveyor belt and people picked the nuts out from the shell. Then the empty shells continued to a sitting dump truck outside the facility.

Pretty cool operation but it does not stop here. I knew that they needed a larger dump truck of the Mid-Liner size. A pickup truck was too small and a big Mack was too expensive. Anyway, I got a good idea. I would provide a demo Mid-Liner dump truck to be placed underneath the spilling area where the empty shells piled up. When the truck was filled, they called me and I demonstrated the ease of driving, as well as how to calculate the weight being handled. I easily demonstrated the value of our product, and it became clear to them how efficient the new truck was compared to the old oversize pickup bed they had been using. I told them not to worry about the shells, as I would dispose of them myself. I drove them to my house and dumped the entire load by my natural scenery beds that had beautiful hardwood trees and dogwoods with gray and white trunks. Then I returned the truck to the factory, as I wanted to get it underneath that spill spot before they drove in their old pickup.

At home that evening I spread those shells in my beds at a three-inch depth and as the beds were being covered you saw the beds come alive, as the deep red color of the shells was effective in making the beds beautiful. A bonus I did not consider, was that although the factory hand-picked all the meat off the nuts by hand, obviously quite a bit was missed and the squirrels had a field day. We would see all these waggling tails in our yard. The neighborhood squirrels were on a mission to get as many as the pieces of nuts as possible before any other squirrel heard about it.

Having taken at least four truckloads for my use, I then convinced the factory that selling the shells was a lot easier than giving them away. Not to mention it was a nice little moneymaker for them. No, they did not buy a Mid-Liner, but we did sell them a used truck from our used truck lot.

As it often happens when things are going well some awful event comes along and hits you in the back of the head. Well, this was like a locomotive hitting you head on. Chuck's daughter, Rebecca, who had just turned 21, was killed less than a half a mile from their house. It appears that the crash did not kill her but she actually choked to death while eating and driving. How in God's name do you, or anyone, handle such a tragedy?

Chuck and his family were loved by everyone that knew them. I remember Johnny, Chuck's son, bugging Chuck for a tree house like we had, and Chuck not having the time to do it. So, one day I showed up with some sheets of plywood and Johnny and I built his tree house. It was not as elaborate as the one I built for our kids, but this was for an older boy and his neighborhood friends. Although it was for Johnny, I knew that Rebecca would get some pleasure out of it as well.

Now she was gone. I have a very difficult time with emotions. Some people think of me as a macho guy, a tough cookie as some would say, but if they knew the "real Franco" they would find out how weak I am in certain ways. I can start crying at a movie theater as soon as there is a touching moment on the screen. There are times, too, when I remember something from my past, and that will bring on the tears. Actually, I think tears are a healthy release of our emotions. But now we were in a crowded room in Chuck and Joan's home with friends, a minister and the mayor of Stone Mountain. What do you say? What do you do? We have no classes to teach us how to comfort others and how to behave in such difficult times. You can only pray to God "Please Lord, make me do the right thing," but the bottom line is asking our friends what we can do for them. When I asked Chuck this question, he replied that he did not know. Even as I write this I am full of tears remembering an event that happened nearly twenty-five tears ago. The feeling of sorrow will never leave me.

I asked him, "Are you going to do a funeral or cremation?"

He replied, "I think she wanted to be cremated, but I don't think I'm capable of making that choice or even talking about it." He looked helplessly at me and again I am in tears writing this.

Chuck went on, "Please make that decision for us, please."

"What if Joan gets mad at me for the decision I make?"

"She won't," he replied.

So I decided to have Rebecca cremated, as it would be easier for everyone. That day was a day that I did not enjoy making a decision. In the past I prided myself in being a decision-maker, but that day I did not want to do it.

In the weeks and months that followed, Chuck and Joan were not the same. Joan was so affected by her daughter's death that she became mentally and emotionally stricken. Chuck worked about the same hours as before, but he had lost some of the zip that he used to have, and that we shared. He did, however, get much more deeply involved in a hobby—flying his own airplane. He went into it in a big way and purchased a used Swiss fighter airplane and had it all refurbished and made this his pastime.

For me it was Bette Ann, the kids, the dogs, the Shriners, work—these things kept me quite busy and an occasional repair call from one of our rental houses more than filled my schedule. In late 1981, having been with Mack over 14 years, I re-evaluated my original goal of becoming president of the company or remaining in Atlanta in the position I was in.

At this time I was doing well financially and owned three homes, a few nice cars, and a red Yamaha. Bette Ann and I kicked it around for a while. She listened to my reasoning and finally she said, "Look, if Mack came to you today and made you a V.P. in any region, would you take it?"

"I guess I'm hooked on the corporate ladder disease."

Not long after this conversation, our V.P., Joe Rosetti, asked me, "Are you ready to move on to bigger and better things?"

"What do you have in mind?"

"There's an opportunity to move to the Bay area, and turn the factory store in Oakland around. We need a good branch manager there." I shrugged and asked, "What's the downside, Joe?"

"Well, he explained, "it would be nearly impossible to make what you make now. But with a substantial salary increase and with the possibility of a bonus or two, you will do quite well. Of course once you prove yourself in this position, you'll be ready for the big opportunities."

He warned me about a few of our employees at that particular branch.

"There are some personal problems in the area of alcohol, I wanted you to be aware of it before you accept the challenge."

This was a really big move. I felt that it would be nice to have Bette Ann on board on this one, as her Mom and Dad would not be able to visit us on their way to Florida any more. I think that she was ready for a change even after making such good friends at Stone Mountain. After I talked it over with her, I found out that I was right. If I was for it, she was too.

So, I sold the first rental house to the people who were renting it, that was good.

Transamerica wanted to take our house over if we did not sell it but I found out that even if I sold it at a deal I would be better off. I got $95,000.00 for it and possibly I could have gotten another four to five thousand dollars if I had the luxury of time but I did not.

The second rental home I gave it to Chuck. I let him take it over as a quit claim deed. At this point I took care of all the loose ends, which took the pressure off Bette Ann. I went to Oakland and met our fifty-two employees, and then scouted around for our new home.

When I returned, I asked Buddy, "Do you want to drive across country with me all the way to San Francisco?"

He said, "Yes, but Mom is not too keen on my missing school."

So I asked Bette Ann, "What does Buddy go to school for?"

"To learn, of course."

"Well, what better learning than to go across our beautiful country first hand and appreciate its beauty, especially in the company of his Dad?"

She smiled, and that was that.

We began our trip by going through Chattanooga to say good-bye to some of our dealers and then our friend Jimmy Maddox at Tri State Mack in Memphis, and headed West on I-40 after that. What an experience this was for eleven-year-old Buddy. Each morning we started out early. I got Buddy up and in the car at five-thirty, and hit the road. He would sleep till about 8 or so and then with a motion with his index finger he would gesture at his mouth, letting me know he was hungry. Then we made a stop to grab some food, and made sure we had gas and went to the bathroom.

Along the way we saw some cool things. I took snapshots with him in front of big roadside dinosaurs and teepees and such. We made sure to call Mommy and tell her of our progress, but we were on a schedule at about eight hundred to nine hundred miles a day. We were moving!

In Texas we saw some Cadillacs buried in the ground with the rear ends sticking out, and you know we had to stop for that. We climbed over the fence to get real close and then I saw a bull not far from where we were, and he did not look friendly—I told Buddy, "Come on hurry!" He had no idea until he saw the bull trotting in our direction, and he put on the after burners and was at my heel by the time we got to the barbed wire fence.

He said, "Dad why didn't you wait for me?"

I told him, "I was trying to draw him away. All you had to do is go away from me toward the other part of the fence." It was a memorable moment and we told Amie and Mom all but the bull part but I am sure that Buddy has told Amie the entire story by now.

Normally we stayed in large cities at night because the motels were cheaper. When Buddy was hungry, we said that, no matter what, the next town, no matter how tiny, we are stopping. As it had a Burger King, we ate and then found a dive of a motel. I never cared to stay in dumps, although I saw no reason to spend a fortune for a shower and a four-hour sleep. If it was a clean looking joint it was okay with me.

Before I called home, I prepped Buddy.

I told him, "If your mother asks for the phone number tell her that you can not make it out. If she asks about the noise (from the trucks going by) tell her it's the TV that Dad is watching. We knew if Bette Ann knew that her little boy was staying in a rat hole she would be quite upset.

Finally we drove through Texas and into New Mexico where there were long stretches and the road went up and down hills that went on for miles. I was driving with the map out, speed control set at about 80 and because there was no one on the road, I asked Buddy to take over the wheel with his left hand while I looked at the map more closely. We were buzzing right along and Buddy said, "Hey Dad, there is a big boat ahead of us!" I looked and sure enough a rig was pulling a good size boat on a trailer, so I told Buddy, "When we get close pass it! He was nervous, of course, and I peeked a little every so often, and all of a sudden as quick as a flash a cop went flying down the highway going the other way.

He turned around and I noticed it, and I threw the map in the back seat and grabbed the wheel while Buddy slid over to his side of the seat. I knocked off the speed control, and brought the car down to about sixty. That cop stayed right with us driving about one hundred yards from our tail, and he stayed there for a few miles which seemed forever.

When we got into California I decided to stop at a motel that looked pretty cool. Buddy liked the heated pool. Fortunately, the pool was open until 10 PM and we had nearly an hour for Buddy to get soaked, and we had a story to tell his sister and mom in a few minutes. We got into Oakland in the early afternoon, checked in at the Oakland Hyatt, as that was where our office manager had made the arrangements.

Visiting the Mack Branch was an education for Buddy since it was in a very tough area, something that he had very little exposure to in the past. I may have shown him some run-down homes in Georgia, but that was about it. Now he was going to get out of the car with his Dad and actually spend time in a forbidding sort of neighborhood. And possibly, in his mind, live somewhere nearby.

We spent some time meeting everyone and also making arrangements for the family's return. One of the regional salesmen lived in Alameda and he said it was a great area and close to our workplace.

Well, that was our mission and was thus far accomplished. After having a nice meal at the Hyatt and a good night's sleep we were ready for the flight home.

California

Chapter Forty-one

I only stayed at the house two more days to organize the logistics of the move and how the car was to be transported and delivered to the Oakland Port as it was only a few thousand yards from work. When I got back I was faced with a number of challenges. The branch was losing money. The branch had two unions, one for the "techs" and one for the parts department. I learned quickly that the unions were tough and the west coast people were different from the slow and easy southerners I was used to. I decided to get settled in the apartment in Alameda first. Then I planned to work out the issues at work.

I was in the apartment in a flash, no big deal as it was just me. It was furnished too, so all I needed was a trip to the grocery store and some time to put my clothes away. Once this was done I called the main union office and spoke to an Italian guy. He arranged to meet me at the Hyatt where I had stayed. Apparently he did not want his people to see him at the dealership.

He seemed to be taken aback by the fact that I was younger and bigger than he expected. Then, that I was Italian and could speak the language well.

I told him, "The techs working at the dealership are milking it for all it's worth, Unless we got rid of some of the bad ones, or turn them around, this branch is going down the tubes."

Stewart stared at me, so I went on. "I did not leave a good job in Atlanta where I was making a lot more money than I am here to see my own future turn to poop out here on the coast." Stewart nodded. He seemed to be taking it in. Then I added, "I want what I do to benefit all of the fifty-two families working at Mack, as well as myself." Looking him straight in the eye I finished up by saying, "You included." Now I am not saying that this meeting changed the world, but it let him know that I was a regular guy and willing to work hard, but he could not play hard ball with me or the place would get shut down.

I had salespeople who were nice guys but not very aggressive. Also they knew little of our new Mid-Liner line. So this was an area that needed immediate attention. If I was going to make positive changes here at this facility it had to happen sooner rather than later, and with everyone's cooperation. We got an extension on our union contract which was good.

I removed every possible thing from inside the service shop, as it was a complete disgrace. There was years of grease build up. With the help of the parts manager, the used truck manager and service manager, we cleaned out this dingy, dirty facility. We sprayed the walls with white paint and put down lines separating the stalls so that you knew where to park a service unit. It was a full weekend but the difference was very noticeable to the workers on Monday morning. I got a picnic table and chained it outside our service entrance, so the techs could eat at a clean table rather than an oil barrel or fuel tank.

We had a guy come in and steam clean the used truck parking lot and he staged the used inventory so that it looked like we were in business. Before I had arrived at the dealership one of our executives had picked up the outside floodlights from our truck plant in Hayward. He asked me if I could get them to one of his friends at Danville High School, as they needed them for the football field. The lighting at the dealership was poor and it was dangerous for women at night during the winter months, so I put the lights up at our facility, and this was another super improvement.

The rear fence was set back from the sidewalk all around the huge property that the dealership occupied, but as we were crunched for room I could not understand why we were wasting such expensive land. I knew if I asked permission from Mack or the city that it would have taken an act of congress to get it accomplished. I had no time for that, I was on a mission. With a chain saw I cut all the limbs that were overgrown and were also in the way, moved the entire fence straight back about ten feet by one hundred and fifty feet long and ten feet by one hundred and fifty feet wide. This became a lot of truck storage we did not have before. We had some theft of tires before the lights were installed, but to make it a little safer I brought Duchess to the dealership. She was very friendly to the employees, but she knew when to look mean and growl at night.

It was now time to find a home for our family. Bette Ann and I picked out a lot on the hill looking out on Mount Diablo in San Ramon. The local gossip was that if you could see the mountain from some part of your house—even an attic window—the lot had a "view," and this meant it was worth much more. Our view was unobstructed, and breathtaking. We paid just over $200,000.00. Then I found a rental home almost underneath the lot we were going to build on, so I knew I could see all that was going on. I rented some cheap furniture until the time came for our home to be done and take our stuff out of storage. We had arrived!

Chapter Forty-two

Finally, we had our rental home at Bolinger Canyon and our new home going up at Mare Lane. Buddy got to go to school at Bolinger Canyon School, which was walking distance from the rental house and once our home was done it would still be close.

Amie's school was Cal High, a large school but a very good one; her bus ride was about four miles.

By the end of the school year, I had the dealership under a new agreement. It was the first time this had happened without a strike or ridiculous increases. I had added a truck pad out front so that we had various trucks on display rather than the way it was—all the stock units crammed in the back lot. I also had our mascot, a gold bull dog, installed at the top of the building. Our flagpole got a good cleaning and I gave strict instructions given in regard to our flag. She was carefully raised in the morning without touching the ground. If weathered or torn, she had to be replaced, and if someone forgot to take her in, then the spotlight was left on all night. I also took personal pleasure installing a waterfall behind our receptionist's desk. The water went into a holding pond that contained a few fish. I also made a pond outside for the technicians to amuse themselves at lunch time. I painted a huge checker board design on our picnic table, providing discarded phone mouthpieces for the checkers. My final project—I had a friend paint two bull dogs, one on each side of the entrance of our service shop and above the doors. He added the cut line, WELCOME TO BULL DOG COUNTRY. I later had street signs made for our parking lot where we had our own Mack Blvd. and Mack Used Truck Alley. The entire dealership atmosphere was changing for the better; you could see it and feel it.

From the very beginning we got noticed and rewarded at head-quarters and we sold more Mid-Liners than ever at this facility.

Management expected this, as I was the Mid-Liner champ, but it took getting the salesmen involved, not just me. I treated everyone with respect and I gave them the proper tools and time and soon there were others hearing about my positive attitude and doing well at their job.

Our new home was a single story ranch of about 2,500 square feet. Soon it was ready for us. For a single story home in this area, it was the largest one. Even though I had to spend a lot of time at work, I planned a pool and had it built in the back yard with a spa designed so I could control the water to go in the spa only or into the pool from the spa. I had it built so that I could do more when the pool people left. I added a massive waterfall with large boulders that went to the water's edge and even over the pool area. Next to the diving board I built a fieldstone topped with flagstone fire pit. It was gas powered and I had a control valve that allowed me to raise or lower the flames. High flames for heat and dramatic look. Low flames for the kids after swimming and for roasting marshmallows.

I created a river too, at the furthest part of our property coming down in a wiggly way to a bridge that I built. This gave the area a Japanese garden look and I had various Japanese decorations in the garden as well as stepping-stones.

The river went underneath the bridge where a well covered pump returned the water back to its source. We stocked it with beautiful Koi fish. At each end of the house was a large deck and along one side I put a large trampoline like the kids had in Stone Mountain. I outdid myself—I sunk it into the ground, allowing me to use the excavated dirt for accenting another part of the yard. I built Duchess a doghouse that matched our home with tile roof and a nice deck. I also made a bocce court with an outdoor green carpet. We played this wonderful Italian game often, and it was always fun.

The back yard had so many improvements and well-placed plants and pigmy palm trees, soon it was the talk of the neighborhood. I also fixed up the front yard. I enjoyed doing these things in my spare time—after all, building and gardening were my favorite pastimes.

One of the perks of the position of branch manager was that we got a membership at Crow Canyon Country Club. This was no ordinary country club. It had the most beautiful chandeliers and when you made a reservation for dinner, there were matches at your table with your name printed on them. The kids did a lot of swimming there, and I took tennis to a serious level and won many singles and doubles championships, although I was still told that my techniques were improper.

Amie reached driving age and we decided to give her the Caddy, and I went out and got a Buick. The Buick was not a glamorous car but with more and more customers that needed to be hauled around or picked up I needed a big four door car and the Mercedes was out of the question as it would send flags up in our business, and the Cimaron was much too small.

As the new year started for Buddy's school at Bolinger I decided to do another crazy thing, so I called the principal and told him that for transportation week I would bring various vehicles to the school for the kids to see. My only provision was that the principal would permit all the classes to participate. I guaranteed him that he had never—and would not ever again—see such an event. He asked me if we should have media coverage, and I told him, "Super idea!"

To set this scene properly you must picture a single-story school of about three hundred kids and possibly ten teachers with thirty kids in each class forming a single line by the curb in front of the school waiting for something to happen. Camera crews are there as they were told that it was a very special event for the Bolinger School and an event never done before.

I had each of our salespeople, used truck people and just about anybody that could drive a truck participate in my happening. I drove the Cimaron for this day as it had the gold bull dog on the hood. I wore an insane red jacket (according to my wife) because it was checkered and the actual checkered figure was a bull dog in various positions.

I had instructed all the guys to follow my car and I had them stop just before anyone at the school could see them. I let them know that I alone was going to drive to the school and park in front, providing plenty of room for others to follow at a later time.

I let them know that when I felt that all was in place, whether teachers or photographers, that I would lean on my horn hard and that was their signal to lean on the air horns and sirens and start driving to the school.

I came to a halt after driving by all the classes and gave out bull dog pins to everyone. It just so happened that the bulldog was also the mascot of the school!

I leaned on my horn to start the vehicles coming. Around the corner came this huge sleeper Mack (you could hear a fire engine siren at full blast in the background as this was going on) powered with a 500 hp Mack V/8. And another full 60-inch sleeper right behind. A Mack Superliner followed. It was bright blue with huge trumpets on top blasting away and 120-gallon shiny fuel tanks on each side. The battery covers were chrome and shined as well. A nine-yard cement truck clean as a whistle was behind that and blasting as well and the barrel was turning. Now they saw the long red fire truck that was the one making the siren sound and it too came up to the school for a lucky child to touch and feel. A Mid-Liner was also part of the mix. A new garbage truck that had never seen a single load of garbage was driven here as kids had no idea that a garbage truck can cost over $100,000. At the tail end was a large dump truck that belonged to a customer.

Once all the trucks parked in front of each class, the salesperson who knew about the unit he drove would tell the kids about it and give each kid a bull dog pin and allow him or her to get in the unit and some would inevitably use the air horn until it ran out of air.

Buddy of course was the hero of his class and no doubt proud of his Dad. We received a drawing from each kid at the dealership thanking us and some showed me with my bright jacket and some were actually quite good. Some were tearjerkers, as no doubt many kids do not get the attention they should at home. More than one came back to me saying that they wished that I was their dad.

Chapter Forty-three

The California move was a good one, but there were some very tragic consequences, which I will soon relate. Basically, the move was an education for the whole family. We were in a new place—California is like no other state—and we soaked up the beautiful landscape and took many great trips.

We saw redwoods that we could drive our car through. We learned by seeing a display of growth rings that these trees went back to the time of Jesus, two thousand years ago. We saw where they burned and survived and could still see the enormous burn cavities. Seeing California is an amazing experience for anyone. Looking back, I think about the various trips across the Golden Gate bridge and touching the enormous cables that magically keep it swinging back and forth twenty to thirty feet in either direction during powerful wind storms, and yet all this is barely felt by the overall bridge and the people going over it. The trolley cars that take you to Fisherman's Wharf and the old fashioned manual bell that is still being used; our many trips to Monterey and the 17 mile drive at Pebble Beach; going to Half Moon Bay and just south of that, visiting the Hearst Mansion and learning of his riches and how he lived. Visiting the Napa and Sonoma Valley, learning how an old Italian family came there, became a world producer of fine wine, Ernesto and Julio Gallo.

We visited Disneyland, Hollywood and, of course, the one-of-a-kind San Diego Zoo. We did a lot as a family and probably more than most. I'm not sure if it was due to my travels or because I felt so much for my new country and could never get my fill of it. In every state and every turn we saw magic. I think we were all lucky and although we had a number of close friends we could have so much fun just with our own family.

I spent as much time with the family as I could, and even when I had to travel a great deal throughout my entire marriage I never once came home and said, "I'm too tired to take you kids out today." My work was my work, and no reason to penalize anyone else.

Now came a time in our lives when Bette Ann and I began to miss a beat. It all began with a neighbor lady who introduced Bette Ann to cocaine. I must confess that my time at work was so intense that I might have missed the change in Bette Ann's manner. If she was really depressed I did not know it. But something must have been wrong in her head because she began a dependency on drugs. This created a rift in our relationship that I thought was just a middle-age thing. But there it was—some full blown marital problems that just came all at once. Even with the love we had enjoyed for nearly twenty years, there was still an unknown hurdle to cross over. How would we do this? Especially, when I did not know or even notice the symptoms of her distress.

Bette Ann had really known only one man in her life, me. Was this a disadvantage to us? We had known ourselves as kids who went from puppy love to sweethearts and from husband and wife to young parents. Then we were a family on the move across the land chasing a dream and enjoying all of it as much as possible. Suddenly we were having difficulties we had never known before. A brief separation seemed to be one answer. I got a lovely place for the family in the elite town of Danville. Maybe, I thought, this would help things along.

One evening as we were trying to sort out our differences, Bette Ann said that at times she could not understand why we had any problems at all. I felt the same way. When she was living in Danville, driving her 450 Blue SL, she had no worries, she said.

"After all, you are still my hero, and such a great provider," she told me.

That statement returned to haunt me countless times.

However, on July 10th 1984, I was startled by two policemen

that came to my door in the middle of the night and informed me that my wife had been killed in an automobile accident. Amie was just behind the officers and she moved toward me, and at the same time grabbed hold of me, and said, "Mom is dead!"

"Amie we don't know that for sure!"

"I am the one who identified her."

I then looked at the policemen and asked, "What am I supposed to do?"

One of them said, "For now get some sleep. You and your daughter need to get some sleep."

"Where is my son?"

The policeman answered, "He's with a neighbor."

I said, "Well, I can't sleep or think about it until I've seen my son."

They were concerned about me driving, but they said to be careful and then they left. Amie and I went to get Buddy, and I thanked the people for watching him, and the entire time as we were driving home I asked them both if they knew what happened and when and how.

Buddy was very upset, as he had had a little argument with his mother before she left and Amie was telling me that her mom had not acted like herself. I questioned her some more.

She said, "For some reason, Mom decided to take my car instead of her Mercedes, and she left some of her jewelry she usually wears at the house."

After Bette Ann had gone, Amie checked the Mercedes to see if it was low on gas, but it started and was nearly full. At home I hugged the kids and reminded them of how much I loved them and that it was going to be extremely difficult but we had to get some rest.

Once they went into their rooms, I started to make calls. I called the police. To get a straight answer was like pulling teeth. When I pressed them they said, "No, I am sorry but we can not release that information right now. You need to call this person or that department."

I finally spoke to a sergeant at the police station and after he interrogated me and found out that I was indeed the husband of the deceased, he finally told me what his preliminary report said. He reminded me that it was *only* preliminary. He said that about 10:36 PM Bette Ann Antonetti drove into the back of a Road Roller (the huge roller machines used to drive over fresh asphalt at road jobs) and crashed.

From the investigation, it appears that no skid marks were found although cones and lights were at the road work scene. She was pronounced dead at the hospital.

Due to the fatality, an autopsy was being performed. Those were heavy words, and as he was speaking, I had a vision of Mom and Fred. The next call I made was to Freddy. I could not call Fred yet. I was scared that I would give him a heart attack, but yet I knew I had to tell him. I somehow thought Freddy would know the best timing, but actually I had no idea what to do next.

I got a hold of Freddy, and thank God, he was not on any mission but was available to talk to me. As I had difficulty starting the conversation, which was the toughest in my life, I knew that he knew that there was not going to be any good news forthcoming and the bad news was beyond his—or anyone's—preparedness. As soon as we talked, he said that he was taking his fighter jet to San Francisco and would be here in a few hours. By morning, Freddy had been at the crash sight, and was by my side. Our eyes were swollen from tears.

As strong as I had been for Chuck, I was worthless in my situation. I said to Freddy, "I really do not know what to do, or who I should go see." We were told to go to a funeral home and that they would assist us in all the arrangements. I am not sure what family members and friends we called, but I was on automatic pilot, not fully conscious of what was going on. Freddy and I went to the funeral home in Concord, very close to the accident scene.

The owners were not nice people. They were so cold, and maybe that was the efficient way to get something done, but I hated it.

"Pick out a casket, flowers, and do you want a burial or cremation? Are you going to have open viewing or closed?"

I wondered, *What in God's name is going on here?*

I finally said, "One time, we talked about cremation, so that much I know."

Freddy said, "I would like the ashes if that is OK."

I said, "Of course."

I picked out this beautiful pink casket even though it was to be burned. I wanted her to be in luxury until the moment she was taken away from me. I would not have an open viewing as they said that she went partly through the windshield, and anyway I wanted to remember her as beautiful as she was, and wanted everyone else to remember her that way too.

Amie insisted that she wanted to see her mother one more time so I decided that, if the family wanted to, they could have a private viewing prior to the normal closed viewing. I talked Buddy and advised him not to have a last look, and he agreed.

I do not know what other details had to be performed, but I know that I had to use two credit cards, as one was not enough to take care of all that had to be done. So many difficult moments came in the next forty-eight hours.

Mom and Fred came—and how do you talk to someone and say that your baby is dead? Chuck was there all the way from Atlanta, and he was probably the only person in the room who had a clue about my confusion and pain.

At the eulogy I spoke to everyone and poured out my soul and I said that although we had a little bump in the road of our marriage, my wife, my best friend and the mother of my children was my one true love, and I had no idea how we would go on without her. I am sure that God had a very good reason to take her at the age of thirty-seven. I said that I had spent more than half my life with Bette Ann and her family and I asked for everyone's support and prayers for us all.

We had people at the house afterwards and again I can not tell you who arranged it or if I did, but it was a blur in my life and I do remember Freddy and me going back to get the ashes in a special wooden box.

My children were seventeen and thirteen years old and I don't know even now what effect this had on them, except that we were all devastated beyond belief. My kids were lovable and cheerful with a great sense of humor, they were both the life of the party, no matter where they went, and I wondered—is this real, or are they hiding their true feelings?

Once this horrible event was over and everyone returned to their houses, the reality came home to me that the Antonettis had to manage without Bette Ann.

Chapter Forty-four

No one can describe the sad moment when you get in bed and you do not hear the usual good night from room to room that you heard as your kids were growing up. The voice of Amie saying, "Good night Dad, good night Mom." Buddy the same, except he ended it, "Good night, Amie".

We took some time off our normal routine, and one good thing, if there was anything good at this time, is that the kids were off school. We moved all the furniture and belongings back to our home. I dealt with all the little things that had to be done: for instance, breaking the rental agreement and after a good bit of persuasion at the rental agency, I was able to get out of it without a ridiculous penalty. This was a time when for once, I was not in the mood to deal.

The Mercedes was in the garage looking like a lost soul. I was not going to let my daughter drive it. I knew that the sooner that car was gone, the better for all of us.

I also knew that Amie had to have a car as hers was totaled. One of our customers admired Bette Ann's car, and also had the money to buy it. The family owned Orlimar, a business that made golf clubs in Oakland. The man's wife was interested in the Mercedes with the personal license plate that said it all—BLUE 450. I drove it to their facility knowing that if they saw it again that the impulse to buy would kick in. They still wanted it, and although they could pay for it, they tried to offer a good bit less than I expected.

I hesitated and the man said, "I'll throw in a perfectly matched set of clubs to fit your physical build." I did not know what value that brought to the table, but, as I mentioned before, I was not about to haggle, so I just said yes, and they were happy and I now had the funds to go out with my daughter and purchase a new

Mitsubishi Galant for her. Not only was Amie my daughter, but she was also the sister and mother to Buddy.

I was most fortunate. Amie was beyond her years. A well-balanced child and extremely mature girl for her age at anytime of her life. Not that we did not have bickering at times between Buddy and her, but when push came to shove, my kids stuck together and helped their dad.

I dove into work now more than ever. You could see that everyone at Mack showed respect or tried to make the load a little easier for me. I got many phone calls from so many people wanting to know the facts. Facts, which, I never really found out. What really happened? Was she shuffling for something in her purse or tuning the radio or did car's light blind her for a moment? Was she just going too fast? We never found out. On some level, I never wanted to.

Chuck and I talked quite a bit, and no matter how I tried not to cry, my eyes filled with tears. I always ended up unable to go on because I was so choked up with emotion. Chuck was one friend whom you could count on, no matter what. As the saying goes, we have many acquaintances but few friends. Chuck was, and is, my friend.

They also say time heals everything, and I know that not to be true. The passage of time makes it easier to deal with a certain incident, but the hurt never goes away.

I now had some real concerns with Buddy. He was caught taking my motorcycle to school. He thought that he would be cool in front of the other high school kids being thirteen and driving a motorcycle but fortunately I was close to the teachers, and one of them called me at work, so I called Buddy at school and told him that I had just been at home picking up some files that I had left behind and I noticed that the bike was gone.

He admitted to me that he had borrowed it. Well, he got grounded for a while but I knew that he had too much time on his hands. Sometimes, at night he slipped out of the window to see some of his rowdy friends. He must have done this a number of times, and probably Amie was aware of it, but since it was somewhat harmless for silly kids to go to the Dairy Queen late at night for an ice cream or to Wendy's for a burger, she thought it was no big deal.

I had the habit of clearing my own mind at times by doing things just as strange. I would wake up at 2 AM, go outside, smoke a cigar and water the front lawn. Or I would backwash the pool filter, or just stand in the backyard staring at Mount Diablo in the moonlight and think about various things.

One night, having nothing in particular to do around the yard, I decided to go to Safeway. It was only a mile from the house in the same shopping center where the Burger King was. I guess Buddy and his friends had sneaked out some time earlier, and now they were skating in the parking lot. It was very late and as I got out of the car to enter the store, I saw the little devil before he saw me.

I walked up to him. He knew then that he was in deep-you-know-what. Without a word, I gave him a nice slap behind his head, and told him to get his ass home. The slap did nothing, but the embarrassment in front of these friends was good for him. In the morning we had a healthy talk about letting me down, and what it meant not being able to trust my own son. He tried to tell me how his friend's parents did not make such a big deal out of it, so why should I? And besides, he protested, he was almost fourteen. I told him that he was right, that the other parents did not think too much about it. However, I did! This talk helped, but Buddy still did stupid things like shooting a BB gun at streetlights, and he got caught by the cops that time. Shooting firecrackers into mail-boxes, and getting caught by the cops again. Driving the motorcycle without a license—and once more, the cops picked him up. Fortunately, the police officer knew me and Buddy too, and that was some help. Anyway, we dealt with it, Buddy and I, and thankfully, got through it together.

Meanwhile, some people at work introduced me to Debbie, a friend of our receptionist. I was not one to do the bar scene; I just never got into that. At forty years old I was not about to start. So when I was pushed into a blind date I shrugged, and feeling pretty lonely, said "What the hell?" So I visited this woman that lived with her mother and father in Freemont, California.

I was greeted by Debbie's mother, a very nice hard working woman who had a job at a cookie factory. My date's dad was working in a warehouse at a large glass company. I learned that she had a six-year-old son and had been through a recent divorce. Now, all of these things should have raised a number of flags for me, but the extremely warm reception that was given to me by everyone was something that I needed.

It's often said that you are weakest at a time of rebound, or whatever the appropriate term is. We dated and got involved.

Amie and Buddy did not put my girlfriend in their Mom's place. Or even a possible step-mom. They were only thinking of dad, and if dad felt better, then it was OK with them. In reality, they were doing a pretty good job of faking it.

I am not sure what made me agree to a marriage so soon, but I agreed to marry in late September of 1985. Yes, only fourteen months after Bette Ann's death, I was planning a marriage. Was it because I still had old-fashioned ideas that unmarried people should not live together? Was it that I used the excuse that this would stabilize the family? Or was it that I needed someone to be with, as I could not remember being alone since I was just a teenager? Whatever it was, my decision was made.

I dealt with my fiancée's former husband and his need to see his son, Tony.

Tony was a nice kid in a difficult situation. He was living with grandma and being transported every two weeks to Sacramento where his dad lived. Apparently his dad was very tight with funds, so no elaborate dinners or restaurants or anything like that. The move for Tony to San Ramon was helpful as now he had an older brother to look up to and also a smart and pretty sister.

Once we were married, my wife's real feelings came out in full force. Her kind attitude towards her new family changed. She became cold and unfriendly to my children, and treated me with much less respect. I put up with it—and so did they—but not for very long.

It did not take Amie very long to leave what I thought was a good home to go into her own world and marry. To this day she says she was really driven out of the house, and that her marriage did not survive because she was not ready for marriage.

In the spring of 1986 I asked Debbie, my new wife, if she wanted to go with Buddy and me four-wheeling in the Golden Hills of the Bay area. Debbie had a 1977 Jeep that was gas powered as well as LP converted, and we enjoyed going "off road" every so often. I had installed the famous bull dog on the hood of the jeep. For whatever reason, she decided that she did not want to go. The place that we went to was actually known as the Oakland Hills. Very pretty area with very expensive homes and an area that if you knew someone that lived there they would allow you to enter this vast area of miles and miles of rolling hills, and some that were more than hills.

We had one of Buddy's friends and his girlfriend in another vehicle going along on this fun trip. Our mission was to go to this place that we had scouted long ago. There was a huge pond with turtles in it. Our plan was to drive around for a while, stop, and have a picnic with the bucket of chicken that we had purchased. All went well as far as getting to the lake and actually capturing a few turtles.

The "old guy" guided Buddy as he got into the muddy pond in his shorts. When I noticed a turtle head sticking up, I said,

"There, no, there" and so on and he did his best to react to my instructions. However, his reactions were slow due to the resistance of the water and the sucking of the mud. The point was that he was successful in getting a few until one time I had pointed out a good size turtle ahead of him to his left side and told him to hurry and get there. He made his turn and started to gain on a large turtle. In fact, it was a huge snake. Once he realized it, he screamed "Snake!" and did all he could to reverse his position. The good thing was that the snake darted at him for a split second, then turned and went away.

Well, this was the beginning of a bad ending. We decided to go four-wheeling, and find a great spot to eat our chicken. We went up a few hills and slowly came down not using the brakes but having the engine hold us back using low gears and four wheel drive. As we got more confident we took more risks going up a very steep grade. Even with the extra-wide, tall tires we started to spin. What happened next is still not clear to this day, but the next thing I knew was that the Jeep was going backwards and I felt it was going to flip on the driver's side. I yelled to Buddy to jump, which he did. He flew out of the passenger side away from the Jeep up hill while I was on the lower side where the jeep was ready to roll. The jeep had a roll bar but it was less structural than decorative.

As the jeep made the start of a left roll I honestly can not say if I jumped or if I was thrown or really what in the hell happened. However, I can tell you that I felt excruciating pain on my right leg as I lay on my stomach on the dirt. I managed to see by the time I looked down away from me the jeep still doing its many flips into what looked like a huge bush. As it came to a halt, I heard a scream from my son saying, "Dad! Dad!" No doubt he envisioned me in the jeep—losing his dad so soon after losing his mother. I managed to let out a low groan,

"I'm OK—I think."

Chapter Forty-five

I was not really sure about the OK part. But I *was* alive. I wondered how it was possible considering what had happened. I looked at the jeep and smelled a fire. I attempted to get up, but had no strength in my right leg. But I knew that this fire meant serious danger. The dry grass was crackling with flames. Buddy and his friend used their shoes and jackets to attempt to put it out, and by luck, they succeeded. I was sore and bruised. My first comment was how pissed off I was because our bucket of chicken was ruined. The only thing that survived of any value was the silver bull dog. We managed to get the car out of there by using trucks and cables, and we got it to the salvage yard in Pleasanton.

When we got home, all busted up and bruised, it took forever to explain to Debbie how I had totaled her jeep. She was accustomed to my playing jokes on her and this seemed to be another. However, once this episode was behind us, Buddy and I started to get itchy (and I mean itchy in places you never dreamt of being itchy) and it turned out we all had been in the middle of a poison oak thicket. I bought out the entire stock of calamine lotion at Walgreen's. But the itch lingered on and left sores, too. I went so far as getting a bottle of Clorox and wetting a rag and rubbing my entire body hoping to reduce this agony. However, this was a small price for the miraculous fact that we were alive. Once again, I wondered about it. So many times I had come so close to dying, and yet every time, something saved me. This time something saved Buddy and me, and I was very grateful for that.

At the same time I was healing my sprained ankle and getting over the poison oak, something else happened at work that made me realize I was not invulnerable. Someone reported that I was "taking advantage" of the company in various ways. The truth was, we all accepted small perks now and then. These included using the Mack paint shop to paint a car, but we always paid for these services. Now, someone—secretly, of course—was reporting that we were always "on the take" for freebies of this kind.

At the same time this was happening, a headhunter agency approached me to be a regional manager for a big fork lift company. I had no intentions of leaving Mack, (I was going to be President, so why would I even consider leaving?), but at the same time I was being "bad-mouthed." The head hunter agency, Korn Ferry out of New York was very persistent and said, "What do you have to lose by responding?" I still put them off, but now I started to feel that Mack was being hypocritical and really ungrateful.

But as fate would have it, the executives at Mack asked me to resign in front of my regional V.P., as well as some other individuals in management. They had asked me to think about it and get back to them. I told them they were all nuts and as a matter of fact, my regional V.P. had had all his kitchen appliances painted in our shop. I was the one who had borrowed one of our Mid-Liners to transport them to the shop, and back to his home. I saw confusion when I brought this up. They discussed promoting me out of the branch manager position and into something else. I stated that I had moved all over the country for Mack. I said I left Atlanta as a favor to the company and lost my wife in the process. Obviously they did not have the power to make any changes and they said that they were going to check with corporate headquarters and advise me accordingly.

To my amazement, they still decided (not sure who "they" were) to let me go.

I was devastated. I had done so much to turn this branch of Mack into a profit-making, progressive firm, and now I was out— and for no reason except that someone wanted it that way. How could this get so out of hand? That certain someone I am referring to, was often so drunk I had to get him out of bed and drive him to work just to save his job. In addition, I had personally bailed some other higher management people out of jail for the same over-indulgence. However at this point there was no use crying over spilled milk. I had never sued anybody, and I feel that our back-logged courts and inflated prices are due mostly to people being "sue happy." But I decided to at least find out if I was crazy or was I in the common term *shafted?* After some depositions, I was awarded a settlement.

Fortunately, the agency that was attempting to get me to have an interview with the forklift company continued to be persistent and I agreed to an interview. I talked them into meeting me in Los Angeles rather than flying into New York. As it turned out they had agreed to meet a number of individuals before my meeting. I was the final candidate, I learned later on. Anyway, I had researched the company so I had an idea who they were and what they did, and I had some idea of the market size they were in. We met and after awhile, they asked me questions in regards to motivating salespeople as well as dealers. The more we talked, the more it confirmed that I was what they wanted. In fact, it was what I had done for years, but this was at a greater scale. The local dealer, Bill Billard, was a real gentleman, and he felt good about me as his representative.

Another candidate had been offered the job, but now was on standby in case I dropped the ball. They informed me that their policy was that although they thought I was an excellent candidate, I had to go to their headquarters in Greene, New York, which is an hour south of Syracuse, New York.

We scheduled the trip and to my surprise I was met by the son of the individual who started this company that started out making cannon balls and ended up in material handling equipment. George Raymond was now semi-retired and had appointed Bill Webber as president and my boss to be, Bob Loderstadt as V.P. in charge of sales.

Mr. Raymond was a nice person and he drove me around the tiny town of Greene, and showed me all the interesting spots. One close to his heart was the school that he had attended and he proceeded to tell me how he purchased it and now it was the training center for not only the employees at Raymond but the dealers and technicians as well.

Each individual could schedule himself or herself and attend the training center. This was a nice thing for me to see at this time, as I needed to attach myself to a new kind of commitment.

I knew that I was being backstabbed at Mack but that did not diminish my love for the Bull Dog. Chuck and I had plenty of long conversation across country discussing this new opportunity. He told me that Mack was crazy to lose a guy like me. He told me that the new outfit would be lucky to have me and possibly there was a good reason why all this happened, and it might all be for the good. So I proceeded to go through the interview process with each individual V.P. in the company. Once I finished the longest day of interviews I had ever had, I returned to the Sherwood Inn where I was staying. It was a colossal looking hotel for the area and it had an antebellum look to it, white gigantic columns outside holding up a large second floor verandah.

The hotel was also the facility used to house visitors and trainees and the word on the street was that each student would get meal tickets for each day at the school and there was no limit on the food that you were able to order once you presented the meal ticket. I had dinner that evening with Mr. Loderstadt. We talked for a good while and he let me know about his sales skills as he had been with AT&T and had plenty of schooling on that subject. Apparently they were very happy with me. They were interested in hiring me right away.

We discussed salary, and although it was actually a little more than I was making at Mack, including bonus, I felt that I could do a lot for them. So I asked for more.

Bob must have had the authority to move on the salary gap as he agreed to substantially increase it. He also went on to explain how their merit system was based on points that a worker or manager achieved. You can make so much as long as you are within that scale but once you reach the top of that scale, the only way to make more money is to change positions. Well now we had a salary that was very good as a starting salary.

The next thing we were to decide was how to split up the country for the regions that were to be appointed. They knew now that I had the experience and could handle the position without much training other than some basic product knowledge.

I would be responsible for dealers from Memphis, west to California as well as Mexico, Hawaii and Alaska. There was another individual in Chicago who took care of the Midwest and North Central states. Another rep handled the East and the Southeast.

The deal breaker was that I was asked to move to New York. I reminded Bob that I was the right man for the job, but it meant a tremendous amount of traveling for me. That being the case, what did it matter if I left from Oakland or San Francisco rather than Syracuse? As a matter of fact the weather was much more predictable on the West Coast. I told him fares would also be less expensive and the efficiency of being out there should be a factor in favor of my staying in the west. He agreed to that and now the only issue in accepting the position was a company car. I told him I had no intention of leaving my personal car at the airport a week at a time. This was a much bigger issue than I anticipated. Bob said that by increasing my classification, he could assign the car. That put me near his status, however. But he said that he would work it out in the next few weeks, and I would be able to get the car.

This was great news after what had just happened to me. Once home, I could not wait the two weeks before I started. I visited the closest dealer that I would be representing in my region. That was the dealer in Palo Alto, Integrated Material Handling. The owner was Dick Briggs. He had been in the material handling business for many years and was thinking about retiring. Visiting him was very good for me as I learned that the Raymond product was like a Rolls Royce in the business of "narrow aisle." This is a term that means utilizing space for warehousing or distribution. The narrow aisle forklift did its task in a smaller aisle due to its design. Therefore you could have more space for storing your product. It is also a forklift that is unique. You are standing while operating it and it is powered by industrial batteries instead of LP or diesel.

I learned about serving the entire needs of a potential customer. As I made my daily trips to see Dick to learn more, he welcomed factory representation as in his words "now we can get something accomplished."

After my second visit to Integrated, Dick was so glad that someone was giving him the attention that he thought he should have had years ago that he called the factory and bragged about the new representative that had been visiting him and how pleased he was that they finally hired someone that knew what the hell is going on.

That rattled Bob at the factory because I wasn't supposed to start for two more weeks. He then rushed the paperwork to reflect the day I first visited Dick in Palo Alto. That way there wasn't any liability. I apologized. My intention was to get a jump on the learning curve and he understood and welcomed me aboard at that time.

So my 42nd birthday was with a brand new company and a dramatic change in my life. I did put in some serious hours between going to New York for no less than a week each month and my whirlwind tours visiting dealers to compile their needs and concerns. I figured once I knew what they bitched about I could see our engineers and discuss it intelligently and the responses would be helpful for the dealers as well as the factory.

To minimize travel, as well as to get the messages out more efficiently, I started a regularly scheduled regional dealer meeting.

The first meeting was in the Oregon territory. We had the host dealer make all the arrangements and as it turned out the first one was in a very large home of a friend of a friend and it served well to keep all twelve people involved close. And kept the costs down too. The home was near Mount Hood and the plan was to have our final meeting there. We got to know each other rather quickly. I was interested to learn that the main competitor was a company called Crown. I compared Crown to Kenworth and Raymond to Mack. Both Raymond and Mack had better products but Crown and Kenworth knew how to market the products and how to wine and dine the customers. We had dealers who represented California, Oregon, Washington, Idaho, Utah, Colorado, New Mexico, Arizona, Texas, Oklahoma, Arkansas, Tennessee, Mexico, Alaska and Hawaii. Fortunately some dealers represented more than one state, so we had no more than twelve at any one meeting so that we could get a lot accomplished.

A funny thing happened when my company car was ready for delivery. It was to be delivered in Hollister, California as the Raymond Corporation had another company at that time in Hollister. I was attending a training class there and they delivered the new Chevy Caprice. I looked it over for just a few seconds and realized that it was not the kind of car that is used in sales. The model was perfectly OK, but it had bench seats like a taxicab and no automatic door locks, and it was equipped with snow tires. It was actually for New York and was not ideal for someone in and out of a car in L.A. or the Bay area. I called the purchasing department that had been buying cars (leasing) for years and the individual in charge advised me how long he had been doing it. I politely told him that I understood, but I need a different Caprice with my specs and I would be glad to do it. It was not easy to get his blessing as I upset the apple cart but it got relayed to me that Raymond would not pay any restocking fee or any additional sum over the existing agreed upon price.

As it turned out an Italian gentleman was the sales manager, and we had a very nice discussion about the car that was just delivered. I ended up getting all the equipment I wanted and a vinyl top as well as power seats, cassette and power trunk release for the same amount of money. There was a procedure problem where the vehicle had a vinyl top and only a V.P. could get a vinyl top. I let him know that no one would ever see it, and it was OK.

I helped train the other regional reps and did some traveling in their territory to critique the way they handled or were handled by the dealer.

In Greene I was known as the guy who smoked cigars outside the Sherwood Hotel. I used to walk nights after dinner up the streets of Greene and admire the homes while I smoked. Over some of the doorways you would see the dates the homes were built. Some of those vintage houses were quite impressive. The town was close-knit and I enjoyed my business visits. I even went as far as to take Debbie to show her my new family of workers. On the Friday that I traveled to Raymond each month I would always bring a few dozen donuts for the group I worked with. To them this was a little unusual until they learned that this was my way of thanking them for providing me with assistance. I also changed a number of procedures that involved traveling. I started out using the corporate travel department but soon realized I could do it better and less expensively than they could. I made all my flight and hotel accommodations and sometimes by talking to the dealer I was visiting and letting him know that I was not there to impress anybody he would help me get a room near the dealership if possible. The main focus was a clean place and a good price. I traveled more than the other two representatives and spent less than both of them combined.

The day came that George Raymond came to me and wanted to spend some time with me one evening to discuss some personal matters. I knew a lot more about him than he knew about me. I had heard that his wife had been abducted, brutally beaten and left in the woods tied to a tree. It was a botched robbery or something like that and it took a while to find her and when the authorities did, it was too late. As it happened, the two of us had each been through an awful experience and I could empathize with some of his feelings. We met at the local bar and restaurant in Greene. I had absolutely no idea why he wanted to talk to me, but I knew I was doing a good job. He asked me to join him at a quiet table away from the bar. He said he had some personal thoughts to share that he did not anyone to hear.

George had two sons. Peter I knew well because I played tennis with him. When he was young, he traveled around like a hippie doing his thing, but now he was happily married to the lady who handled warranty claims. George had another son named Steve who had been jumping around from the parts division, to the carousel division and when I first met him he was in Hollister, California in a position that I did not know much about. According to the rumor mill Steve had a difficult personality and had a hard time getting people behind him. So now it appeared that Peter could care less about getting a dealership or becoming president, but Steve wanted to move up and follow his father. George asked me if I could assist Steve in running the Bay area dealership.

"How can I handle two jobs at the same time?" I asked him.

"Well, you would need to quit your present position and work with Steve at the dealership."

I told him that I did, in fact, have experience doing that.

"I don't think Steve can do it alone. But with your help, he might be able to pull it off."

So George proposed that under the normal policy Raymond would have thirty percent of the business. But in many instances I would get nineteen percent and Steve fifty-one percent. This was a tough decision, as I had to literally quit what I was doing in order to accept it.

I spoke to Steve about it and asked about how much money would be involved and he responded that he had no intentions in using any of his personal money and that Raymond would be backing it.

Next I talked to Debbie about the job offer. My constant traveling was hard on her and our relationship. We had also decided to try to have a child with the hope of getting closer and having fewer arguments about Tony. So, my method of having a baby boy was back in service.

I wrote my letter of departure and next thing you know I was in Palo Alto in the same building where Mr. Briggs had his dealership. I learned that he was about to retire and had been given a very fair settlement.

The rebuilding of any dealership is difficult. You have some customers use you with stories of past deals that you know nothing about, and you also have customers who have been lost and you do not know why you lost them. You have employees that do not understand why you are the new sales manager rather than them and they tell you they have been there since Adam and Eve.

Chapter Forty-six

T he cleaning of the facility included everyone ...
Buddy, Tony, and Debbie. We had a name change, which
sounds like nothing, but changing every service vehicle was a lot of
work. Everywhere there was a logo that had to be changed. I had
to deal with existing sales people, ordering equipment, new as well
as used. Evaluate and readjust the pricing of the equipment, as it
was not realistic to real street value. All in all, it was a very
challenging task. But measurable results are what feed me, and
what keep me motivated.

We had our own regional meetings without a regional manager. We included the spouses every other time so that the women
would also get some benefits of their husbands traveling, but it also
created a nice harmony between the wives and it made the meetings
with the guys much more productive.

I now celebrated my 43rd birthday with another company, and
now 1988 was approaching.

Over the course of the next year, things went sour in a number
of ways. Many times Steve and I attempted to discuss our agreement
of ownership, and each time a delay came up and there was some
kind of excuse. Personally I felt that I was being taken advantage
of. My value to Raymond was worth more than the nineteen
percent ceiling that had been fixed on my worth to the company.
Steve felt that the nineteen percent was too much. My understanding
was that it was meant to be a starter, and would go up from there
as results came to fruition. Discussions with Steve led to a parting
of the ways, but it was Steve's doing, not mine. To make a long
story short, Steve felt it would be better if we parted. Well, that
went without saying. So I returned the company car I had at the
time and my 44th birthday was spent receiving my last check from
Raymond Handling Concepts Corporation. I was relieved, in one

way. Steve had no clue about sales or running a dealership, and once I had turned things around, he wanted me out of there. Now I had some time to reflect on my future.

We had a baby on the way and I hoped this child would lessen the friction that existed between all of us. You never have enough money in life, but if I had to, I could manage to cut back, even sell our home that had escalated quite a bit in value, and maybe I could afford to retire and just do consulting or whatever came up that interested me.

Buddy was trying to convince me how important it was to have a brand new car and that was perfectly all right with me. But then he needed to have an immediate change to the sound system and modification to the speakers. He assured me that if I would float him a little loan that not only would he pay me back but also he would have such a great car that he would keep it forever. What a load of malarkey. But he was my son, and I had done plenty of foolish things when I was his age. So off we went to the Sound Store in San Francisco to get ripped off. Two thousand dollars later we had boom booms and tweeters and who knows what else. No more trunk space and a good bit of the rear seat gone but we had SOUND! They called it sound. I actually could tell when Buddy was coming home as a certain part of the sound vibrated the whole house. Of course he was not alone in this craze.

I am not sure why things happen in bunches, but not long after my parting from Raymond, I learned that Chuck had lost his son, Johnny, to a motorcycle accident not far from where Johnny's sister died. Chuck did not notify me until all the duties were over and Johnny had been dead for nearly a week. I think that Chuck knew the difficulties I was having at home and he was not going to add to them even though he himself was at the breaking point. How can you describe what a true friend he really is? Except by saying someone who is always there for you.

Not long after that Buddy decided to join the Marines. I was surprised, as it seemed to me that this was totally out of the blue. But apparently not. The recruiter came to our house and we discussed how often Buddy had spoken to him, and how he thought that Buddy was level-headed (could have fooled me) and that the Marines would give him a better focus on life. I had a difficult time accepting all of this, but I remember saying that I would be proud to have a son in the Marines. I recalled Fred saying how proud he was of his son being a fighter pilot in the Air Force, and now he was in the Navy as an instructor in the landing of amphibious boats. My last comment before signature was this: "Buddy, once we sign, I will not be able to get you out of any problems if they should occur."

He nodded, and was proud to join.

Before long Buddy was off to San Diego for training, and as luck would have it, Amie accepted a promotion from a large telephone company where her main duties were to sell phone contracts to new companies. So, I was not worried about either of my kids, but, for awhile there was myself to think about. What was I going to do now?

One thing that came up was a job offer—at one of the Raymond dealerships I had serviced. One man, Chuck Martiny, was doing all the work for this company in Phoenix, and he needed some help.

I knew from previous experience that Martini, as I called him, was in not only financial trouble but he was not performing to the level that Raymond expected their dealers to perform, and to achieve market share.

I told Martini that since our new baby was due shortly, I would just think about it, but I knew for sure that I had no intentions after the last go around with a Raymond dealer that I would work for someone unless I was part owner. If that opportunity did not present itself, I had no interest.

Finally we were ready for Adam Troy to be born in Hayward, California. Once more my system worked—a healthy boy was born on September 9, 1988. His private parts were normal and now we had two boys living at home, Tony and Adam.

Buddy was shipped off to Camp Lejeune doing a six-week training. A quick fix to anyone who may have been a discipline problem. Buddy was never that, but he was not shy about doing some dumb things. Now he had a mental and physical challenge ahead of him. I knew from experience that I had prepared him well for the physical part, and I knew he would enjoy the competitive training.

One evening while Buddy was in training, he called me, and said, "Dad, they want to cut my testicles!"

I said, "What are you talking about?"

He answered, "My testicles turned blue and they were going to do surgery on me, but I told them I had to call you first."

"Get me whoever is in charge!" I actually do not remember exactly who the individual was, but I do remember that the conversation went something like this. "Look, I am Mr. Antonetti and my brother-in-law is in the Air Force and one of his sons was disfigured by one of those goddamn Air Force doctors that performed a circumcision and if you guys screw up my son I will do whatever it takes to destroy you. You better make damn sure that whatever you do is the right thing and not some half-ass short-cut as I will have my people look at it after the fact."

The individual at the other end of the line assured me that they were well aware of the seriousness of their actions, and would only operate if it was absolutely necessary. As I understood it Buddy had had his testicle twisted and was lodged and this caused a loss of blood that might lead to gangrene and even death.

For whatever reason, Buddy did not get operated on and his problem was resolved without an operation. This was a great relief to me.

Chuck Martiny called around the same time.

He said, "I understand your concern and I am willing to entertain the idea of some type of partnership, if our working relationship turns out to be compatible. How does that sound to you?"

I said, "I am willing to come to Phoenix and work out some type of strategy in getting your company turned around, Chuck. Then we can work out exactly what our individual functions would be."

His reply was that we would discuss everything in more detail once we met.

I actually commuted, believe it or not, as for me driving has never been an issue, and the same held true as far as sleep—I only needed a little to function normally.

So I flew down to Phoenix and made up my mind about whether to give this a shot, mainly to see if Chuck and I could get along Monday through Friday. I also wanted to find out how many hours I could handle without being inefficient. On Friday at 5 PM, I left in my rental car for San Ramon, California—722 miles away.

I could usually do it in eleven hours, if the weather was perfect, and in twelve hours under not-so-good conditions. I would rest until about 8 AM, and I was as good as new. Projects got done that needed attention and I spent time with Adam as well as Tony, and it was all pretty manageable. If this had to be forever, I do not think I would have considered it.

I left on Sunday, taking some personal items, clean clothes etc., and usually my departure time for Highway 5 by way of Tracy was after dinner. By 6 PM, I was on the road. I was at the apartment at 5 AM. After a nice shower, I was ready to roll. Sometimes, I got a catnap before leaving the apartment for work, but I was always a stickler about being on time. I would be upset if I was not at work prior to normal working hours. Any employee that was always late would drive me up a wall and would be confronted with a one-on-one private conversation saying that if you can be seven minutes late every day you should be able to alter your schedule to be 7 minutes early every day. That is, if you cared for your job.

The cold facts were that the company was on COD with many vendors, the sales force was quite lazy, and no one person can do all that is needed to run a dealership. You need discipline and you must not deviate from certain policies. No doubt it was tough for Martini to give up a portion of his company. In his mind this was his baby. In reality he would be losing not a portion of it but all of it if something was not done, and done soon.

So, I took on the role of Vice President of Sales and Service. I think the title was more for the new or existing customers to realize who I was. I was prepared to scrub the restrooms if that was what it was going to take to turn this dealership around. You can quickly pick up trash, paint the walls and even replace carpeting. But until you fix the financial stuff, things won't get better. Banks only understand ratios and bottom lines. My actual words to Martini's wife, Mary Ann were, "In a short period of time, if I am left alone to run my part of the company, I'll make you guys millionaires." She smiled and said sheepishly, "I hope so."

Arizona

Chapter Forty-seven

We had been together for a few weeks and I knew that under the conditions we discussed that I could make it a go. Not only get results but also have fun doing it, especially once I moved the family to Phoenix. The only obstacle was if Martini got greedy and refused to let go of a reasonable part of the company. He had agreed to a seventy-five percent Martini and twenty-five percent Franco arrangement, but I did not feel that it was enough.

I told him, "If I have to kick in some money to inject the cash that the company needs, I will do so. However, less than thirty-five percent ownership will be a deal breaker."

In the end, we agreed that I would help out with some cash and the ownership would reflect Chuck sixty-five percent, Franco thirty-five percent.

So now the new project was to sell the old home and find a new one. I was more concerned about getting the new one, as I knew that the Bay area home market was always pretty good. I did not want to wait months to get into a new home in Phoenix, as it would mean more driving back and forth.

I decided to look at Scottsdale. Although it was pretty far from work, driving did not bother me. If I got to work by 6 AM traffic was no problem. I was the last to leave in the evening, so again, no traffic.

I met this nice Italian builder named Tony, and he was in the process of finishing a wonderful home in the Powder Horn Ranch subdivision in Scottsdale. The house was probably thirty days from completion, but it was custom and had features that I had not thought about before—sub-zero refrigerator, roof tiles that were installed three thick with mortar in between. The look was unique and added to the quality of this ranch-style Italian-design home. Once finished we would have a play pool, gazebo, outside shower and BBQ area and the whole thing completely landscaped with fruit trees and, of course, the required fig tree if you are any type of Italian. The home was probably the largest that I had ever purchased, and possibly the most expensive home that I would ever buy. Who ever thought that this immigrant kid looking for wallets in New York nearly thirty-five years ago could qualify for a home that was over $350,000.00. Not only did I qualify but also with $200,000.00 down, the purchase was really affordable. The San Ramon, California house sold for $375,000.00 (At this moment it is up for sale at $675,000.00)

At this time Buddy graduated from basic training and we went to visit him at his base in San Diego to be part of the ceremony. You should be able to spot your kid in an auditorium, however, the only Marines that were a little different were the ones with dark skin, and everyone else looked cloned. I could not find Buddy as they all were sitting down with their hats on, and it was impossible to see under those lowered brims. Being the person I am, always doing silly things, I walked up the stage and with my right hand over my eyebrows to help me see into the audience I said, "Hey Buddy!" Well, I guess he was told to remain at attention because I saw no movement. However after what seemed a long time, a Marine next to him pointed Buddy out to me, and at that time I could tell my son by his smile *and* his embarrassment.

Amie, Adam, Tony, Debbie and Buddy's best friend, Keith from San Ramon were there. And a number of other individuals that Buddy kept in contact with. We had a nice time and he was allowed to go off base and I took them all out to a nice dinner. He was then transferred to Twenty Nine Palms. This was pretty lucky for us, as it was only about five hours from our home. Twenty Nine Palms is one hundred percent dependent on the base, and quite close to Palm Springs, California.

At this time there was not much going on between Bette Ann's Mom and me. Losing her daughter was extremely hard on her. As much as I knew Mom loved me, she had once said that if I had not taken her all over the country she would not have died. Fred still cared for me, but his wife of nearly 50 years was his concern, and he was not going to upset her in any way. He chose to keep his feelings about me to himself. I would hear through Amie—as she kept in constant touch with them—that Fred would tell her stories about me, and all of them were positive. Often Mom called Amie Bette Ann, and Amie was smart enough not to correct her, or even think about doing it.

My own mother, on the other hand, was trapped in New Jersey until the day that Grandma would die. That day finally came, and of course, I was the only one at the time who could do anything for her. I flew to Jersey and since Grandma's funeral was prior to my arrival, my mission was to sell the house on Garfield Street. I contacted a real estate agent and explained that I wanted the house to sell fast so I could take my mother to Scottsdale.

We worked out a quit claim deed giving my mother on a side draft over $150,000.00. We traveled to her bank getting all the customary bank accounts that Italian people often start for every person that they've ever met. One grandchild had $122.35, another had $352.90. We closed them all and I was to get them to the proper individuals or their parents, depending on the age. Some of these accounts were twenty years old and the deposits that were recorded were deposits of two and three dollars, in order to keep the accounts active. We gave away so much stuff, but most of it was not worth moving.

The item that she most treasured was this very large Italian doll the size of an eighteen-month-old baby with porcelain face and legs that I had to carry around all the way to Scottsdale.

The actual walking around at the Newark airport was very

revealing for me as my seventy-eight year old mother who was always extremely strong, seemed to be walking with a great deal of pain, and had to stop every ten yards so she could rest. The problem with most Italian old people is this—you can tell them you have a broken finger, and they answer, "Yeah, you have a broken finger, you should see my broken arm." And if you have a broken arm, they say, "I have a broken neck and only one eye." It is like a card game, "I will raise you one arm and one leg. You raise me two stitches and a bump. I have four stitches and a cast." So I was not alarmed by her slow walk, as it could have been the start of one those impairment games. Anyway, I finally got her to Arizona. Of course, the first thing she said was—"Oh, I can't breathe! I'm going to die. I can't get off the plane, just the walk from the plane to the airport is too much for me."

After she had rested I decided to have her hips examined by a physician. I am ashamed to say that the doctor said, "I cannot believe that this woman actually walked by herself. The one socket is destroyed and the other is very bad." I scheduled my mother at Scottsdale Memorial Hospital and magic was performed, and although it was extremely expensive even with supplemental insurance, it got done. I saw to it that she put her feet in our pool, and enjoyed Adam and me when I was home.

After my mother was with us for four or five months, I started hearing stories. My mother and Debbie were like day and night. I had a job that was demanding and I needed to keep my focus centered on it. We were making good progress but I came home at night to a lot of bickering. After the operation, we kept getting astronomical bills because thousands of dollars were not covered, for one reason or another, and I made the calls dealing with duplication of charges, or whatever the problem was. One specific bill was for "counseling." The statements showed $185.00 for this service. A few days later another bill came showing the original $185.00 due, but now an additional bill from the same doctor for another for $240.00 for consultation. I called and spoke to the receptionist and asked her to explain these charges. She went on her merry way with a cute story of how concerned the doctors were and how they sit next to their patients and let them know what is expected of them in the rehabilitation process, and how they will be helped every step of the way, and how they answer any specific questions that the patients may have.

I asked, "Does the doctor speak Italian or English?"

She laughed a little, and responded, "English of course!"

"So you are saying that the doctor does not speak Italian?"

"That is correct."

I advised her that if she did not reduce the bill to zero, I would bring this to the board's attention.

"My mother," I told her, "speaks only one word of English— SONOFABITCH!"

Naturally, we did not receive another consulting charge.

To save what marriage I had left and to go forward with my mission at work, I called my brother Aldo (you have no idea how painful this was) and asked him to take mother to Las Vegas, so she could stay with him for a while, at least until I knew for sure what I was going to do. He, of course, was most interested in mother's financial picture. I believe he was relieved when he learned that she had all her money, less a few thousand dollars that went toward medical bills.

I told Aldo, "She'll come to you with her finances intact, and I have no intention of getting involved in that area, I can assure you."

So mother went to live with my brother and his wife and then I heard all kinds of stories about her buying his house so she could live there, and how she lost her money, one way or another. I will never know the truth about how any of this really happened, but at least there were no more unpaid bills that I was responsible for, and she did have a roof over her head and someone to care for her. It was time for me to focus all of my energy on the dealership.

Chapter Forty-eight

Martini and I decided that we should buy the building that housed our company. So, we approached the owner and he was agreeable to turning the rental into a purchase at this time. We started an LLC partnership that was 50-50 and that was the first positive step in getting the company into a good cash flow situation. The company would now pay a fair price to rent the building from our LLC. It was nice to see the enthusiasm that I created for the entire company by moving a ribbon that I hung on the rafters way up high in the warehouse. Every other month the ribbon was moved to the rafter in front of it. This showed the progress that we were making to buy the building. At first it seemed insignificant, but as time went by you could see the ribbon's progress and that we owned nearly fifty percent of the building. That was a big deal.

One weakness we had at the early stages of our turn-around (besides cash flow) and not enough sales was that we needed a gas line, a line of sit-down forklifts, a line that allowed us to quote outside forklifts for tile companies, lumber companies, nurseries, and our own rental department. We got a little luck when we found out that TCM did not have a dealer. They were, however, looking for one. After a few visits, we came to an amicable agreement and we were their dealer for Arizona. Their headquarters was out of Texas and our relationship turned out to be a very good for both of us. We increased our customer base as well as our rental fleet and now we were actually calling on some new customers that, in the past, had nothing to talk to us about.

We felt some friction from the Raymond Corporation, as they were concerned we would neglect their line to market another. We proved ourselves and increased our market share in all categories. Customers do not want to train every vendor that comes to their door and they welcomed a single source outlet that would learn their business and provide to them all of the equipment they needed.

Having the new line increased our parts sales and helped enlarge our service department, and all of that was good. We now decided to get a greater line of credit at the bank and I had to personally guarantee my property to secure this, as Martini did not have sufficient equity.

Now, we were starting to cook. I began to order used equipment that was desperately needed. I used my personal checks with many wholesalers, as our company credit was either weak or not established. I was overly concerned about money; I was concerned in making the company successful at all costs.

The building, although it was built to Martini's specs, had some problems. One thing was the gray carpeting on the entire lower level of the office, as well as the parts department waiting and counter area since we had technicians walk in the same spots as potential new customers, who came in for one reason or another, and the carpet was filthy from all the grease. I therefore had some nice Italian tile laid throughout the entire lower floor. I even tiled our conference room since we had our meetings in there with the entire company. Suddenly—with the new tile—the place brightened up, and there was no more telltale grease because the floors were easily cleaned. Wow, we were starting to look good!

I came up with an idea to get us noticed not only by old customers but potential new ones as well.

We announced an event that was to be called a Material Handling Extravaganza.

Contacting every vendor that worked with us, I let them know that I was thinking of having their product displayed at our Extravaganza. However, if they had any interest in participation they needed to set up an area that I would designate and they would be responsible to staff it and do their sales pitch. I also expected them to have novelty items to give away. I provided all the invitations and the details of follow up—name tags, games, food, beverages, and the clean up of our facility prior to setting up the equipment.

We had a huge turn out and the beauty of it was that the customers learned about us informally. Some just came to play and get prizes, but that was OK too, as now they saw our facility, and knew what we were all about. I also got to see some of our competitor's salespeople, and they got to see me, and some came over for a job, and one person is still there today.

As the ribbon moved, we also provided our people with other incentives. A 401K plan was started and the company would kick in twenty-five cents for every employee dollar. We rewarded personnel for not taking sick days and we also provided cash rewards.

We began an employee of the month program. I had plaques made and it's funny but in the bottom of each plaque I placed a gold bull dog as added value, and each month not only did that individual get praised at our monthly meeting but he/she was also given a personalized cake. The award was also written up in the monthly newsletter that we started. I wanted everyone to know all the good things that were happening at Handling Systems. The final part of this award was a pull in the raffle bucket where you drew a number at random, and got a chance at winning two hundred dollars.

I brought donuts, bagels, and various pastries, each and every Friday, no matter what. If for some reason I was out someone else was assigned to do it. I bought a beautiful grill. The day before I was to fire it up I announced a "pot luck" for the next day. In the morning I got the grill ready for sausages, steaks, hot dogs, ribs. Many of the employees talked about what they were bringing and we ate lunch in shifts, and it was enjoyed by all, including truck drivers or anyone else that happened to be at our facility.

We were more than a company—we were a growing family. And our competition was disappearing, one day at a time.

We also began a tradition of a company picnic at a park that we all had a part in planning and we encouraged bringing kids and I made sure they had plenty of prizes and fun. For the grown-ups I attempted to teach some of them the game of bocce. The women participated as well as the men and everyone had a ball. We did the same at Christmas, and to make it less expensive for individuals to attend and bring a present, we asked them to get something no more than ten dollars in value. If it came from a woman it was wrapped in pink; and if it came from a man, blue. It was simple and when it came time the guys would go to the blue table and grab a present and the girls would pick one from the pink table. I made sure that my present was always an expensive one so that I would get a surprised reaction from the individual who was lucky enough to pick it.

Our company was becoming well respected and our credit with vendors was allowing us to purchase equipment by just asking. The vendor knew the bill would be paid in a timely fashion. The best reward for being in good grace with vendors was that in some cases you received a two percent discount if you were in good standing. That was big bucks when you calculated the overall volume we were doing.

I now received a call that I did not expect. It was from Buddy at Twenty Nine Palms. He was not allowed to say much other than that he was shipping out soon. We all had our noses in the TV news for the past few weeks so we were aware of the unrest in the Persian Gulf. The idea of Marines going over was not a surprise, but it became a reality when my son was involved. Buddy was in the tank division and I thought of how gung ho he was, and, as a kid, how accident-prone. Well, if something were to happen over there, he was going to be in the thick of things. I knew immediately that I had to make a swift trip to Twenty Nine Palms to provide whatever support I could give. In truth, he did not belong to me anymore; he belonged to the Marines. It's hard to describe what went through my mind in my lonely five-hour drive.

Debbie did not want to go and her excuse was that I needed to be alone with my son. In a way it might have been a good idea as a number of times on the way there I broke down with tears that I could not control and they say it is healthy to get that emotion out of your system. For sure, I could not have done that if someone else had been in the car with me. I cleared the security gates once I announced who I was and the purpose of my visit. The base was loaded with parents who were as concerned as I was, and, of course, each child is just as important as any other child. How ironic that I use the word "child." Children they were to me. Most were teenagers and yet these were the individuals that we were about to release to fight for our rights and precious freedom. The same kids that could not drink in most states could indeed give up their lives voluntarily. Certainly food for thought.

The moment came when these kids attempted to throw that heavy canvas bag with their worldly belongings into a holding area that would later transfer them to a bus and eventually to a transport plane and then to an untold destination. My son was gone! I now had to drive back home and I had no reason to hurry and, as a matter of fact I was so empty that I could care less about my arrival anywhere.

I did not go home that night. I was more tired mentally than physically, but anyway, I decided that my office was a better spot at this time. Employees at work knew that something was not right as I was never late for work and I never entered without a big smile or a pat on someone's back as I walked by. But today they sensed that something was wrong and even I could not hide it.

Eventually I opened up to Martini and a few of the management staff, as well as a few old friends like my buddy, Chuck, in Atlanta.

The remainder of the war was news, news and more news. I hoped for a glance, some mention of that kid who was my baby boy. As concerned parents we made packages and sent items that we knew were important. We packaged biscotti and other Italian goodies that Buddy could share with his Marine friends as well as items that we had heard that they needed like flea collars, (turned out not to be true), toilet paper, and lots of letters and photos. I did not realize that my son was madly in love at this time and had been with his high school sweetheart, Jen, and most of his letters went to her, and understandably so, I might add. What seemed to be a lifetime of waiting, hoping, praying finally came to an end. Our son was coming back. The war was over.

Chapter Forty-nine

We were very lucky that Buddy came back safe and sound and with a medal. I knew that many others were not so fortunate. And it seemed to me that my lucky charm or secret angel was now visiting my son as well. Once Buddy was back at Twenty Nine Palms, we all went to greet him and I got to meet Jen. I am sure I had seen her as a kid when we lived in San Ramon, but I did not remember it.

Buddy had grown up in such a short time. He still had a goofy personality like his dad, I might add, but now he was thoughtfully planning out his life, and I could see that he had goals. The day came, not so long after he returned, that Buddy wanted to get married. Debbie and Buddy did not get along, so I now became the wedding planner. Not to mention chief financial backer for the program. I was going to take care of the rehearsal dinner as well as the flowers and whatever else was customary. Jen's mother worked as a manager of the facility where the wedding was going to take place.

I asked Buddy where the facility was because I did not know.

"Off Hagerberger Road," he answered.

"You mean the road that goes to the airport?"

"Yeah, you got it!"

"Buddy, there's nothing there but that triple XXX motel, you know, the one with questionable clientele."

Sheepishly, he said, "Well, Dad, that's where Jen's mom works, and it's not that bad a place."

I told him, "How can I go to a place like that especially with your grandmother and your sister? What if the staff shows up nude?"

Buddy went on about how Jen's parents could not afford to go anywhere else. And he added, "Besides, there's a famous harp player who works there."

"In clothes?"

"C'mon, Dad."

"I can just see her playing ...."

"By the little lake," he finished. "Yes, it's going to be beautiful with floating candles during the ceremony and no one will know that it is a place where you would not go unless—"

"Yes, Buddy."

Well, I knew we were going to handle this whole thing as carefully as possible. What would Mom and Fred think? I knew they were coming, and I did not want them to be embarrassed by the front desk and its ample display of devices, batteries and speeds.

I called one of our good friends who ran Francesco's, a super Italian restaurant near there, and that took care of the rehearsal dinner, which went as well—or better—than expected.

The wedding day came and it too turned out well.

My biggest surprise came when I learned that Amie was to be married for the second time to an older gentleman—someone I had not yet met. Or even heard of. The plan was to get married in Monterey—no family, just a few close friends. I had a hard time accepting that I was not going to be present. But, on the other hand, what could I do?

Anyway, Buddy's wedding went—I can't say without a hitch because that was the point of it all—but the kids got married and Amie's wedding, minus Daddy, followed.

So now the kids were married and my company was doing more than ten million in sales, and everything was working out except my own marriage. That was going badly.

Plus, as I was spending more and more time at the dealership, I did not really know how badly my marriage was going until the moment when it fell right into my lap.

Sometimes in life, or in business, luck guides your every move. How many times Martini said, "I'm so lucky to have you!" But now a really fortunate thing happened for both of us. The local Nissan dealer was going out of business, and I decided to take over his program and do it ourselves. The first disagreement I ever had with Martini came at this time. He did not think that we should take on Nissan, but rather take on Cat, another heavy equipment line available at the same time. I had plenty of experience selling against Cat in my days at Mack, and somehow I managed to convince Martini that this was not the way to go. So, in a short time, we were the authorized Nissan dealer as well as the authorized Raymond dealer of Phoenix. To me, this is like saying you are the authorized Ferrari and Rolls Royce dealer. Not just some guys selling and servicing forklifts. All at once we were undisputedly number one.

I have been blessed with my children, but in addition I can honestly say that, for the most part, my children have been blessed with me. Which is to say—we talk to each other as much as possible and we work things out together. Now Buddy came to me with some new ideas about his future. He wanted to open a large equipment company in the Bay area. We talked about it and I threw out a lot of questions, and he and Jen came back with their own answers. In the end, however, they decided to move to Phoenix where Buddy would come to work at my company, and I could also help him buy a new home.

The first thing I told Buddy when he came to work was that he would have to work harder than anyone else. He started with the worst job and that was to steam clean the forklifts outside. The conditions, owing to the heat in the summer and the cold in the winter, were tough. Plus there was the grease that had to be cleaned up. Buddy did his job without complaint, though. I guess it was easier than the Marine training camp.

Jen was also a hard little worker and she made pretty good tips as a waitress.

It was not very long before they dragged me to see the perfect home in Chandler, Arizona. We visited the site with a realtor and we went through the home. In Buddy's and Jen's eyes, it was perfect. But it took me just a few minutes to let Buddy know that this house was a joke—badly built and in an area that was losing rather than gaining equity.

I showed him the cheap hollow doors with only two hinges for support. I pointed out that the house was facing east and west, when in Arizona it should have faced south with the back patio to the north. I explained all the reasons why the house was no go, and as I spoke, Buddy listened, and something clicked. Finally, he smiled in agreement. Jen, however, did not smile; she frowned. Well, so be it.

We finally looked at a home, which, again, was no go, but next to this one was another that was a single level 1,800 square foot home on a nice lot on a quiet street. The price was reasonable. I discovered that I could do the upgrades on it myself. Still, as it turned out, Buddy and Jen were told they did not qualify—this without the company doing a proper credit check. I returned with them and after clearing up the error, Buddy and Jen ended up the owners of their first home on Erie St. in Chandler.

Once again my life went back to normal. Things continued to go smoothly for me in business. But they were not working at all with my marriage to Debbie. Sadly, things fell apart faster than I could patch them up, and in the end, I did not want to do any more patching, so we called it quits. Suddenly I was out of my own house and living in a motel. It seemed that just as my children's lives were coming together, my personal life was falling apart. I was starting all over again.

By now Buddy and Jen were in their new home with plenty of room as I helped them with various projects but they had no idea that I was this close to kissing my marriage away. So I called Buddy and told him that I had moved out. Then I asked him, "Could I use that Ford pickup to move some of my things from Scottsdale?"

"Of course—but what for? Dad live with us, please. We have a huge guest room that is just sitting there and plus you are always at work, so we won't even know you're here, and on top of that we like your cooking so you will be doing us a favor."

With that, Jen came on and confirmed that I would not be interfering with their lives and she would be glad to have me.

That was all it took; I accepted.

So the next thing I knew I was living with Buddy. He opened up to me and said how difficult it had been living with Debbie. She was a lot different when I was around, he told me. He said, too, that when Amie got married the first time, it was mostly to get out of the house. Well, that was a tough thing for any Dad to hear. I thought it was a shame that Debbie had made enemies of my children, and finally, of me as well.

My divorce took quite a long time to resolve, but I had made up my mind that whatever it cost was a small price to pay if I had peace of mind and my kids back. I gave away the home that I liked so much. And the equity that the home had made plus all the improvements—that all went to her.

To facilitate the divorce proceedings, I granted her everything that was in the home, too. That is, everything I had collected thus far in my life. I also gave her twenty thousand in cash so she would have something extra to live on, and I paid all of the lawyer's fees on both sides. My son's child support came to over eight hundred dollars per month. I did have a prenuptial agreement, which Debbie had signed, but her lawyer said she had signed it under duress. I let it drop. In the end, I settled the entire matter in an expensive way but that expense gave me freedom that has no price tag.

While living with Jen and Buddy I noticed that my son was always broke and I knew that he had just moved up to a warranty and dispatch, and was making pretty good money.

As Buddy and I worked on various projects at home and work, I tried to tell him in a nice way that between both of them they should be living really well now. I told him I did not understand the financial problems they were having, especially since Jen often said how much money she was making in tips at her job. What was happening to the money?

Buddy answered, "Well, we charged a lot at Sears and I got a tool box from Snap On, and Jen got stuff for the house."

"Is that all?" I asked.

He looked a bit vague, and didn't say anything more.

"I think you need to look a little more closely at where the money's going right now."

He said, "Sure, Dad, I will do that."

For the moment, we left it at that. But I sensed something else was wrong.

Unfortunately, not long after this conversation Buddy had more problems than finances. He soon confided to me that his relationship with Jen was not as true as it should have been. She was, as it turned out, cheating on him. And the next thing I knew was that Buddy had begun his divorce, and since his was a relatively simple matter, he concluded it before mine.

I was dumbfounded and grief-stricken at the same time. Here I was living under their roof, and did not know what was going on any more than Buddy did—until he found out the truth. As a dad I felt miserable. Did I have something to do with this broken home? I mean, by moving in with them and adding an extra burden?

Buddy swore this was not the case. He said he and Jen had been having problems for quite some time, but they had kept it under wraps. "I need to move on with my life, Dad," he explained.

So, now, we both lived as bachelors in his house in Chandler.

We went to work together. By five-twenty, I was in the car ready to roll, and we were at work before six. We were usually the last to leave. But that was nice, we had no after-work schedule, and some times we ate dinner at Rigatoni's restaurant. Our favorite was clams in a broth with wonderful Italian bread to dip in it and the house salad. What a wonderful meal, and one we still enjoy today.

All in all, the two bachelors were doing okay.

On the work front, the dealership was growing all the time. I started a profit chart for the employees to show them how they were faring. It was displayed in the warehouse on a large 4x8 piece of plywood that I had drawn, something like you see when a united fund drive is advertised and they show you how much of the goal has been achieved.

Our company had made a commitment to the employees. We set aside a percentage of the profit each month and at the end of the year, we distributed it equally to any employee who had been on board since April of that year. So when someone walked into the shop and saw $8,356.00 as the amount to date, they could do the math, if they wanted to. Let's say it was September: already each employee was getting $225.00 at Christmas.

One day I bid on a service job that required thirty Raymond forklifts. The customer could not afford to buy new ones and decided to go with our older equipment—but he also wanted it to look as fresh as possible. I provided a re-build quote that I knew we could live with, but the customer then gave me an unrealistic delivery time to get the forklifts updated, painted and tuned. I said, "I don't see how anyone could deliver that soon." His answer came quickly, "If I give you an additional week will you guarantee delivery?"

I knew that all things being equal, we could handle the time frame. But, what if some of the parts were delayed? I decided that it was too big a job to pass up, and I agreed to the critical deadline. The following morning I went to the guys I trusted deeply and let them know that I had made a difficult but good decision for the company.

"I've accepted an enormous challenge to get this job done," I told them. "Now I don't pull on wrenches like you guys but I will do anything to help, including helping out at night or whatever it takes. If we can manage to make this work, it'll be a nice feather in our hat as well as more profit for everyone, and you guys won't make a liar out of me."

As it turned out, we had nothing but cooperation and we met our deadline and no workmanship was compromised. I thanked everyone from the bottom of my heart. Then I said, "I need one more favor, and that is to tell your spouses that I need them the following night for a meeting at the shop. You're going to be late getting home. I'm sorry to ask for this on so little notice, but I need everyone to attend."

The next night we had a huge lobster and steak dinner at our cookout facility, and all the employees were there with their families and everyone had a great time, except maybe Martini who was never fond of spending money in that way. I always told him, "To earn money you must spend a little." But he did not see it that way. All he said was, "Where is mine?"

I told him, "Well, you and I don't need this—it's for them. They earned it."

Martini stammered, "But—I am the president of this company and I am paying for all this stuff, so where's mine?"

Fortunately, I think this remark went unheard.

The next bright period in the history of our company was when we outgrew our 39th Street location. We needed to find a larger building. We called some real estate experts and explained our basic needs, a roughly twenty-thousand foot square foot building. We wanted to look at land as well. In the end, we found a three-and-a-half acre property next to the 10 freeway near 24th St. As soon as I saw this I was sold, but Martini found every excuse not to buy.

So we climbed back in the car and proceeded to look at another site. Everyone got out but me. I remained in the car. The realtors motioned to me come along, but I refused. Martini came back to the car figuring that I was feeling ill. "What's the matter?" he asked.

"I'm okay.

He said, "Hey, let's look at this one."

"I found the lot I wanted, and I am not looking any more. If you want to look, go ahead but I am done looking."

Martini did not look happy at hearing this.

Well, granted, I have my shortcomings. But when I think I am right, my stubbornness really comes out. Maybe that is good, maybe it is bad. But that is what I am. That is the way it is.

So now we had a big discussion. Martini thought I was going to bankrupt the company. I told him I had a vision. "If ever there was a money-making location, the lot I picked is the one." He gave in finally, but not without fuming. Later on, when the blueprints were being drawn up, Martini was always sighing and saying, "You're going to break us." Well, we had a huge celebration and press coverage the day that we had our ground breaking. Our bankers were right by our side and they knew they were doing something right. I did, too. My vision was holding true.

Chapter Fifty

Martini felt that since we did so well in getting the old building paid down, we should think about renting it out. I thought we should sell it and buy used forklifts. I knew we could make a great profit doing that and in the end my logic got through to him.

So now our company was a major force in the state of Arizona.

Buddy and I were fortunate to be able to do projects together at home. We landscaped the backyard in an unusual and creative way. We planted miniature citrus trees and we sunk a trampoline. I created a waterfall and a pond with submerged colored lights. A six by three-foot wide fire pit dominated the center of the back yard. Our next project was the requisite bocce court, which we finished in grand style.

I would pick up my son Adam and all three of us would do projects and sports, as well as go out to dinner, or learn to make Dad's sauce that literally took six to eight hours to prepare. Adam, even at five, was self-confident and appreciated spending time with his Dad and older brother.

Amie had started her family and now I was a proud grandfather to a wonderful little boy named David.

At the second Material Handling Extravaganza I got to meet the mother of Melissa who was working in our service department. Her mom's name was Teri. At the picnic we played volleyball and I got to know her a little better. A few more accidental meetings and we decided to have dinner at her house. Melissa lived there too. We had a great time although she reminded me that I was a little too forward. But I was just being me and I had no intention of making her feel uncomfortable. We saw each other quite a bit after that.

As luck would have it, the house next door to Buddy went up for sale. When I saw the sign go up I told the owners that I would buy the home. I had no storage in Buddy's house and this would be perfect. He said that the real estate lady was to come over shortly anyway and that she would talk to me.

She came over to see Buddy and me that night and talked about the price and I agreed to buy it after they reduced the price slightly. She said, "Before we sign the appropriate papers let's go in the house so you know exactly what you are buying."

I told her, "I don't care what's in the house. All I want the house for is the garage." She gave me a baffled look.

I said, "Look, I have no intention of living there. I'm buying the garage to store my cars, a boat, and whatever else Buddy and I have. I expect to stay with my son in his house until he finds someone with whom he is serious."

She shrugged, and said, "OK."

So, in a short time, Buddy and I were father and son, bachelor roommates, and neighbors all at the same time. His address was 1921 Erie and mine was 1931 Erie.

Our next project was to knock down a portion of the wall in the back yard dividing the two properties, as in our mind, it was one. So we cut the blocks and made a cute gate.

Time went by and I saw Teri often. She and Adam got quite close. He really looked forward to our doing family things. Anyway, since we were now three additional people at Buddy's, we decided to use the house next door. Now, of course, there were new projects. After all, it was a home not a garage. Yes, another waterfall. So there were now two quite different waterfalls splashing away and then I had to plant a few fig trees as well as some citrus.

Teri had a very pretty white American Eskimo dog and Buddy had a trained Rottweiler that failed the police test because it was not mean enough. These two loved to run from Buddy's yard over to mine and vice versa as long as we left the gate open.

Teri and I were living together on a sort of permanent basis, so I helped her with a quit claim deed so Melissa could own Teri's old house. Teri had been married for some time. She had two children from this marriage: Melissa, who was nearly Buddy's age and Kenny, who was a few years older. Anyway, it was nice having all the kids live in the same state with the exception of my daughter Amie who was in California.

We had a nice family get-together one weekend and we invited Amie, her husband, Dennis and our grandson, David. The idea was to show them Dad's new home.

I explained that Dad had lost the home in Scottsdale and that it was going to take some time to recover from that financial loss. "Don't expect a mansion," I told them.

Well, the really great thing was that Adam was finally going to meet David.

When I thought about it, it was funny—a little kid like David calling another little kid his uncle. But that was the way it was, and is.

When Amie, Dennis and David finally got to Buddy's they were exhausted. They had a long difficult drive, but they arrived safely. I decided to play a trick on Amie and told her to get back in the car and follow me to the new house, as I couldn't wait to show it to her. She's a good sport so she agreed, reluctantly, and we drove around the block and pulled into the driveway of my new house. She looked really confused when I jumped out and said, "We're here!" This is still one of our best jokes.

As the family started to reunite I also kept in touch with my mother-in-law, Mary or Mom. She really liked Teri. Amie would plan for Mom to stop in Phoenix for three or four days before going to see her in California, I felt so relieved that she could feel good about me again. We even discussed a family vacation like we used to have years ago. We worked on trying to set it up for Disneyworld, since it was close for her and her son Freddy and all his kids and grandkids.

I told Amie that I would take care of everything as who knows what can happen and I wanted to enjoy my kids now. I wasn't concerned with leaving any money behind. I made arrangements for six round-trip tickets to Florida. I figured on Teri, Franco, Adam, Buddy, Amie and David. The kids wanted to stay at the Wilderness. You can rent a mobile home for a week that looks like cabin in the woods. We let Mom know and she would do the same and this was going to be our family vacation for a super week.

Unfortunately when I called Debbie, she made every excuse imaginable as to why Adam could not go. "No way are you going to take him out of the state," and so on.

So I had six tickets and five people. We decided to give the extra ticket to one of Buddy's girlfriends. So that was the plan and everything got confirmed and as the days drew near we were all pretty excited. Not so much for Disney but for Epcot, River Country, and other things we could do in Florida. Then, a few days before we left, I got a call from Debbie. "Adam can go," she said.

"What?" I said.

"I've decided Adam can go after all."

No reason given, just a decision she had made.

Well, to tell the truth, I was fed up with her unreasoning ways, and I just said, "I'll think about it." And I did. But, in the end, Adam did not go.

We had a wonderful time anyway. Buddy rented a six person golf cart so that we could jump on it and not wait for the tram to take us to breakfast or the pool area. We visited so many parks and ate at so many wonderful restaurants that the kids are still talking about it.

Once back home I managed to get Adam the following week. I told him that we wanted him for the summer, or at least part of it. Teri and I started to do a bit of traveling ourselves. She had not traveled at all in her life and my travels had always been business-related. So this was going to be just for us.

I bought a nice Riviera and got special plates that read MR LIFT. I had left the Bull Dog behind as my new life was forklifts. My employees called me Mr. Lift, Franco, or if they pointed me out to someone, they said, "That guy with the big cigar."

All things considered, I was feeling pretty much like my old self, with a life that was truly worth living and the people close to me having the good life as well. But the thing I did not realize was that Amie was having some serious problems with her son David, who was suffering from allergies and had quite a few serious reactions having to do with cleaning products that Amie was using in the house. Amie was concerned that I would think she was either not spending enough time with David or that she was doing something wrong as a mom. So I was unaware that David was having serious attacks. It was obvious when Amie finally called me (as she usually did before making a serious decision) and told me that she was going to quit AT&T and go full time into the natural soap making business. She also explained that she and Dennis were already doing this part time. In addition, she had decided to get rid of anything in the house that was not chemical free. In short, Amie was on a mission to reroute her own life and to save David from his chemical sensitivity. The soap making inspiration was a direct result of her thinking about natural ways to treat her son.

"You know, Dad," Amie said over the phone, "the soap I've been making and selling has really helped us, and a lot of other people, too. So many women have written me after trying my soap blends. They're all amazed at the results, both in cleaning and getting rid of reactions like David's."

I told her, "Well, you've got to be pretty brave to jump into this home business just like that. I mean you have a big salary at AT&T, and you've won many awards there, too."

"Dad, if I do not jump in with both feet, it's not going to work. A sideline company is doomed for failure."

I had to agree with that line of reasoning. "So, what are you going to call this company of yours?"

"Soapworks," she said.

And—just like that—I knew it was going to work.

After I got off the phone, I told Teri what was happening. She looked a bit doubtful.

I said, "Amie's a gutsy kid and although she's not really a kid anymore she still is a fighter and with that attitude they will make it."

Teri and I had been together for a few years when I decided it was time to consider getting married. I asked if she felt the same way, and she did. I belonged to the Arizona American Italian Club in Phoenix and they did wonderful catering and special events for various people, so I inquired and found out that they would be glad to host our wedding. Teri felt as great about this as I did, so it was all set.

We invited Chuck from Atlanta, and Al and Kay Shaw from Memphis because they were our closest friends from out of state. The wedding and ceremony was wonderful, and we danced the tarantella, and everyone had a great time. Chuck had bought "throw away" cameras and he gave one to David and one to Adam, and they had a ball being the wedding photographers. Strange as it may sound, they came up with some wonderful shots.

So now we entered our cute little house as Mr. and Mrs. Antonetti.

On July 17th 1998 I was 54 years old and on the 18th of July I was again a married man.

Chapter Fifty-one

Now, it seems to me that whenever you save a few bucks, something happens. Something that causes you to spend the funds that you thought you had. This type of problem happens a lot when you are young. It is different when you are older. The difficulties I am talking about came right after our marriage. We, Martini and I, had grown our forklift company at an impressive pace. But this had taken a tremendous amount of my time doing all kinds of things that I did not like to do. I would follow up on receivables, for instance, and discover to my dismay that only when we were a little short on cash was there an effort on the company's part to collect.

Most of the time my plate was so full, I could not—and did not want to—put anything else on it. But there was Martini, always finding more and more things for me to do. Things he did not want to do at all. Now we had had a ten-year relationship and partners are no different than marriages, as far as I can see. We had gone to our limits, the two of us. I am sure he did not enjoy my getting so much attention from our clients who always called asking for me. It must have been shocking for him to find out that some of our customers had no clue who he was.

I am not saying that Martini did not play a role in the growth of the company. He certainly did. But when the company was a breath away from the abyss, he did not know what to do with it—and I did. I had carried it through a difficult upturn, and now that the company was quite successful and my promise to make the Martinis millionaires was fulfilled, Chuck was very short on work and very long on criticism.

Actually, the situation was quite simple. I retired from HSI with an amicable agreement between Martini and myself. So, now Teri and I had the time that we had wanted to use for so long. We were finally home free.

We decided to have our home built and we moved to Gilbert, Arizona in 1999.

We sold our cute home next to Buddy but before closing we had to close up the gate area that allowed us to go back and forth, and, for Buddy and me, that was a sad moment. But deep down we knew there would be another gate somewhere along the line, and this, too, has come to pass. But I am getting ahead of myself.

Buddy was now in a good relationship with Shirley, who had a twelve-year old daughter named Brittany. As a matter of fact, Shirley and Brittany lived not far from our new home in Gilbert, although they were spending more and more time at the home in Chandler with Buddy and Sam the Rottweiler.

Buddy told me he was talking to Shirley about getting married, and possibly building a new home. I did my best to let him know that a child from another marriage was a lot of work and took a lot of understanding from all parties concerned but especially the child. I could say this with a little bit of confidence as I had experienced it.

So this is no small task and I told Buddy that, and he agreed. Well, it only took Shirley two seconds to find an acre lot in Queen Creek to build their dream house. They were excited to show Teri and me the lot and how excited they were. We all said that it looks like a good area but it's pretty far from work.

Bud said, "It's close to Shirley's work and the view is worth any amount of driving." Before you knew it Shirley got possible builder's plans, models and prices. She even started looking for mortgages.

Teri and I were just getting ready to go to on a cruise that began in Athens and went all through the Aegean Sea.

When we returned we looked at the plans that they were very serious about. I was shocked that they actually had gone as far as they had in what I called a pipe dream.

I had to be careful, but I had very strong opinions about what they were planning. The house was way too big, and they were paying $50,000.00 to build a basement and in doing so losing a bedroom upstairs.

I looked at Buddy, "What the hell are you going to do with a basement other than to raise spiders and store junk."

"Well, Dad, I thought we could have a game room." I explained that he could have a fourth bedroom for the same money as the basement. He could also add on an additional garage to use as a play area. We changed the design and the square footage and found it was possible to build a lovely home on the land that they thought they could afford, even though I still thought it was much too much.

Buddy told me that I always lived beyond my means and provided the family all the luxuries that others didn't have. And he was following in my footsteps.

"Buddy, you're not me. You get bored easily with projects."

But at this point they were very set, so Teri and I agreed to help as much as we could. They decided to sell both their houses through an agency. Then they would walk away with their belongings and any equity would be lost. They were living with us and for Shirley's daughter Brittany, it was good since the school she attended was close. Buddy and Shirley now could bank the money that they had previously spent on mortgage, utilities, taxes and as far as that goes food, as we were now willing to do all that was needed so that they would have a huge down payment to facilitate making a reasonable balance and smaller mortgage payment.

Buddy and Shirley were planning their wedding and they had the idea that they would get married in the front entrance of their unfinished dream home. One of our vendors turned the skeleton of a house into a wonderful room with drapes and backdrops.

A lot of carpet was laid over the dirt leading to the front double doors that were not yet in place. A friend of Shirley's made a lovely cake and the same vendor that provided the backdrops brought in chairs.

I felt kind of sorry for the neighbors. Buddy's motorcycle club attended with their rumbling Harleys. There had to be at least one hundred of them. I was extremely concerned. The last biker to pull up was the one who was to marry Buddy and Shirley. I thought nothing could top the ceremony at the Triple XXX motel, but I was wrong.

Buddy, Shirley and Brittany stayed with us until they moved into their new home. It wasn't really finished, so I helped them finish it up. We tiled the floor and accented the whole house with more decorative tile. Then came the landscaping. An acre is a lot of property to landscape with a low budget. We did it with perseverance and hard work. It was a slow and tedious task, and Buddy kept saying, "We'll never see the end of this."

I told him, "Your problem is that you're spending too much time looking at how much more we have to do instead of admiring how much we have done."

We did manage to do it and because we did it in small sections we made the walkway curve so nicely that it flowed and enhanced the look of the front yard.

The back yard was the next step. The hardest part was putting up the six-foot block wall that went around the entire property. I made Buddy's back yard level with lots of truckloads of dirt and then I installed a sprinkler system, so now we could plant whatever we wanted.

The overall project took about three months. Just as we were laying the last stone in place, I started thinking about going on a nice vacation. That was the day Buddy informed me that he hated driving to and from work.

He said, "It's too far, and as a matter of fact, I'm thinking that Shirley and I are going to separate soon."

I scratched my head and stared at him. "Am I hearing you right?"

"Well, the marriage isn't going so good."

I still could not believe what I was hearing. I told Buddy that Teri and I were there for him, but maybe he should give this a little more thought.

Within a short time Buddy was back home.

One evening Buddy noticed that I had a spot on the side of my neck that I could not see. I had Teri look at it and she said that she had seen it a few weeks ago but was not sure if it was her imagination or if it had always been there. So I went and had it checked out. Dr. Allison informed me he did not like that mole. He sent me to a specialist who seemed to know what he was doing. He looked at the mole and said we should schedule an appointment to remove it the following week. That left me with a lot of time to go really wacko with my thoughts. Well, no doubt I was quite nervous. The doctor sent out the biopsy and said he would get back to me with the results in five to seven days. More waiting, more crazy thoughts.

On the fifth day I got a call from a nurse. She alarmed me more than was necessary, I thought, by her impersonal manner. She informed me that the affected area was larger than the area that had been operated on. So they would now have to do another, more extensive operation. Fortunately, when I spoke to the surgeon he calmed me down by letting me know that this was quite common. and that he just wanted to be extra careful. Following the second operation, and waiting another five days, I was advised that everything was fine. I was OK. Once again, I felt that I had beaten the grim reaper, who was always one step behind me.

For a moment—just a moment—I thought I was in the clear.

Then I talked to Amie who was greatly relieved that Dad had survived the two operations and was all right. However, she seemed to be holding something back, and when I asked her what it was, she told me, "I'm not doing so good with the soap business and it's affecting my marriage to Dennis. I don't know how much longer he and I are going to be together."

I sighed, and said, "Well, the Antonettis don't seem to have much luck with marriages. You know, your brother's ending his second marriage, and I just finalized my divorce, and now I hear you're maybe going to end your second marriage. No, we're not lucky when it comes to getting hitched, that's for sure."

"Dad," Amie said, "if the pressure of the company and our financial problems were not so great, who knows, maybe we could save this marriage."

I was more alarmed that she was having soap company woes than I was surprised at her having marital troubles. Actually, her company was in the news. I had many national articles on Amie and her Soapworks. She was in the National Enquirer and Time Magazine and I had seen her on Extra and other major TV shows. How could her business be failing in the midst of all this good publicity? As we talked further, however, I learned that it was the same old thing—cash flow. So she was paying her vendors at a very slow pace and this had greatly affected her productivity.

"You know, Amie," I said, "cash is king."

"I've heard you say that before. It's easier said than done."

"Not really," I answered. "My solution is this. Move the operation to Phoenix and I'll help you out. I know a lot of the chain stores and I can assist in getting your product on their shelves. Moreover, I can run the warehouse and the distribution operation. Lastly, if you have overdue bills, I can pay them and get you back on your feet."

There was a moment of silence on the telephone, and then Amie said in a soft voice reserved for difficulties, "Dad, we owe a lot."

"How much is a lot."

"About two hundred thousand dollars."

"That's a lot, all right."

Now the silence was on my end. But I told her, "Look Amie, move it down here, we'll get started right away."

"What about the debts?"

"For the present, I'll carry them—personally."

Amie was speechless. I told her to start thinking about it and to talk to Dennis right away.

In short order, arrangements made to sell the home in the Bay area and within a few weeks, Soapworks was in Phoenix and I was managing it. I got a warehouse from a company called Odorzout. The founder was called Dr. Stink and he helped us into a good new location. Then I met a woman who was locally known as The Queen of Clean on Channel 3. The Queen got Amie on her show, and I got soap into Basha's, Safeway, Albertson's and all the other big commercial food chains in the Phoenix area.

As fate would have it, I became the forklift operator who unloaded our product and I filled individual orders. In short, I did the job of the thirteen former employees who had haunted Amie's failing business in the Bay area. Who knows how much money we saved by having one man do the work of a half dozen?

When I was not working for Amie's company, I shared free time with Buddy, and I finally found out where his life was going, or not going, as the case might be. Buddy had gone ahead with the divorce, as I had suspected he would. The unfortunate part was that although they had acquired a lovely lot and built a beautiful home that was nearly finished, the whole thing was a disaster financially. I learned the sad truth from Buddy. He had actually paid someone to take over the payments on the house because he could not afford them.

The good news was that we were all together.

What a wonderful luxury that was, too.

The rest, no matter how scary and crazy and full of vexations for everybody, could be worked out in time . . .with the help of Dad.

Chapter Fifty-two

So my only disappointment at this time was my relationship with my son Adam. He was now nearly thirteen years old and his mom would not allow him to contact me. The court stipulated that I was to have weekly visitations as long as no disagreement arose. I knew if we pushed the situation Debbie would somehow make Adam suffer. We knew that as long as the child support was paid every month Adam was all right. It was frustrating not to be able to see him, but for the moment, there was nothing I could do. I was not about to get into another legal struggle with Debbie. Time would tell if Adam was stronger than his mother.

Kenny, Teri's son and his wife Marci, were trying to have a baby but we did not know that Teri's daughter Melissa had fallen in love with a nice guy named Russ, and that she was trying as well. So now we were going from one grandchild, David to—who knows how many grandchildren? Marci and Kenny had a baby girl, Alexis. Melissa and Russ had a baby girl named Hailey born ten days later. Then a few minutes later Hailey's sister Taylor came into the world.

We had a larger family all of a sudden. Three girls.

It was nice seeing Amie all excited with Marci as well as Melissa talking baby talk and all that gooey stuff. So Teri and I had to re-learn the whole parenting procedure—no sleep, diapers and checking on the little ones to make sure that they were breathing.

All the hard work that Amie and I were putting into Soapworks was finally beginning to pay off. Amie and Dennis had a number of good opportunities but luck and timing are so much a part of the success of a business. In Amie's case she was fortunate to meet Jeff Wycoff, the founder of Zap, one of the nation's most successful cleaning products. Zap became popular through well-placed infomercials. At first, however, these infomercials did not succeed—not until he put himself into the picture presenting his own product, his own way. Then it really took off. Jeff had seen Amie in various venues when she was promoting Soapworks. Of course the name he knew her by was Amilya, her professional name.

Anyway, Jeff spoke to Amie about Soapworks and his own interest in the company. Mainly, I think he saw her star potential as a personal promoter of her product. In fact, he saw a way to help someone else along the ladder of success in the same way he had come up. Amie told me about this and I said we should go to Los Angeles and speak with Jeff about a possible merger. We left my home in Gilbert about two in the morning and were in Jeff's office before ten AM. We had a very open discussion and I had talked to Dennis prior to going and had a pretty good idea what they wanted to do. Soapworks being so short of capital, needed another boost, and Jeff was the one to do it—if he was interested and if Amie and Dennis agreed. As it turned out, he was, and they were. This was a favorable situation for everyone. We made an agreement with the understanding that Dennis had to accept the deal or it would be off the table.

Fortunately, Dennis saw the benefit of Jeff's entrepreneurial magic and his money, and the deal was finalized in short order. Now I felt like my real retirement might start on course, as I would no longer be needed as a shipper, invoicer, packer and sender of Soapworks. Everything was working out perfectly—or so I thought.

The moment I thought things were at stasis, I found out that Buddy wanted to get another house. We looked at the area he liked and for some reason he was working with this real estate agent that may have been feeding him a little too much bull manure.

The home was a two story and the numbers did not add up. The upgrades that Buddy called for were not included in the down payment, and therefore the house was too expensive for him. I switched the focus to a house that was equally nice, but one he could afford with his salary and the savings he had made by living with Teri and me.

Finally, Buddy found a great lot and we picked an affordable house. While it was being built he had another six months to save and to reserve money for a nice down payment and materials. This respite gave us time to arrange a wedding for Melissa and Russ— better late than never—and to review the contracts for Soapworks.

Just as everything was going smoothly—another monkey wrench. Really, it was another extension of angelic hands. What happened was this. Teri and I were driving in Amie's Durango when we turned off Highway 10 going west. I glanced in my rear view mirror and saw a car coming on uncontrollably. I knew we were about to have a terrible collision. I yelled to Teri, "Hold on!" It was another of those moments in my life when time stood still and everything happened in slow motion. Then I snapped out of it and I cut the wheels to the left in order to climb onto the curb. I wanted to run up the hill away from the exit ramp. Even with this attempt at escape from disaster, the oncoming vehicle struck the rear left part of the Durango and spun us around like a top.

Teri was hysterical and crying. She had been thrown against the passenger window. I was bleeding from my forehead and I suppose I was in shock. Miraculously, we had each survived the accident with minor injuries. But I believe I was up to a least my ninth life. The vehicle looked bad, but it was still drivable.

"Teri, are you all right?" I asked.

She whispered, "Thank God that you were paying attention." Then she added, "I think you are blessed."

I shrugged but I knew deep in my heart that my angel was still looking after me. That and the fact that I would not die. Well, looking in the rear view mirror in the nick of time had been the decisive factor. If I had not done that we would have been crushed.

Fortunately we were both well enough after the accident to spend some time with Al and Kay, our good friends from

Memphis. Teri still had some aches and pains, but the chiropractor helped to relieve them. As for me, I had another small dueling scar to go with some of the earlier ones.

I had not seen Al for some time. Now when I looked at him he was different. It was not his age; it was the fact he had lost so much weight. He almost looked like a different person. Kay said that he lost almost fifty pounds and he had done it by himself following the Atkins diet.

At that exact moment I decided to do the same thing. So I gladly gave up pasta. But not the braciole, the pork chops, meatballs, sausage that goes in it. I gave up potatoes, bread, rice of any color, milk, sugar, fruit and I even cut back on carrots. Drastic? Maybe. But I decided that at 260 plus pounds I could afford to be a little on the extreme side when it came to what I ate. The truth was, I had not been able to bend down to tie my shoes easily and my clothes were getting tighter and tighter.

My routine now was walking every other day first thing in the morning around our block at a good pace. The block was just over 1 1/2 miles and I would eventually do it in 20 to 24 minutes. I had no real problem with the diet as I am like a machine once I decide to do something.

I did all the shopping because I enjoy it, plus it gave me a chance to make sure that all the stores I visited had the Soapworks products. If it was not displayed properly, I adjusted it. If I had a yearning for a snack, I ate little Italian salami or a piece of cheese. Every night my splurge was, and is, five almonds. Not six or four but five!

After three weeks I had lost 12 pounds and I was at 248. Suddenly the whale was under 250. A few months later the whale was a 240-pound marlin. By the time we decided to take our road trip on June 15th 2003 I was down to 231. I had lost 29 pounds, nearly two bowling balls in less than five months and felt better than I had in a long time.

Chapter Fifty-three

We started Teri and I, by going to Williams, Arizona, and playing it by ear after that. As it happened, we stayed overnight and in the morning took the train with the glass dome windows for the top passengers, and went to the Grand Canyon. There we had a great time and after lunch, we came back to Williams for another stay. The following day was a loosey goosey adventure as we headed for Bryce Canyon. From beautiful Bryce we drove on highways 12 and 14—breathtaking—and saw Sedona for the first time. Then we ambled up to Jackson Hole, had a nice stay there, and ate at Bubba's. Yellowstone followed and there I felt sad seeing the result of the forest fire of 1988. It was depressing to see so much destruction, like viewing the site of Mt. St. Helens. However, the park, geysers, buffaloes, elk and all the other animals, the clean cold water and the mountains, reminded us what a great country we live in.

We headed toward Mt. Rushmore where I had to go off the path for a while to see Devil's Tower. If you saw Richard Dreyfus in the film "Close Encounters of the Third Kind" you understand why I wanted to see the Tower, which is a stunning site to behold.

Still, I expected it to be larger than it was. Movies make everything larger or smaller, I suppose.

After this we went on a mission to visit southeast Iowa where our new son-in-law lived prior to coming to Phoenix. We drove around the area and took plenty of pictures and then drove on to see Al and Kay in Memphis. When we phoned them, they were at Disney World with their grandkids. We told them that we would see them on the way back, but they would not hear of it. They asked us to go to their river house in Arkansas, so we accepted. Then we drove from Ohio to Arkansas, stopping at various casinos along the way.

At Al and Kay's cabin, as they call it, we had the luxury of no less than four bedrooms and a 3,000 square foot space with a deck that goes nearly around the entire upstairs level looking down to the swift waters of the Red River.

We fished and fed the raccoons that visited in the evening and would not leave until all the food was gone. Their favorites were marshmallows and fish. After a few days of relaxation, we drove on to Collierville, which is outside of Memphis.

The new house left us with our mouths wide open. A mansion in brick Southern antebellum design, massive yet also friendly and inviting. Kay was anxiously waiting for us in the front yard when we pulled in. We skidded to a halt in front of her driveway, as we were excited to give her a big hug. Kay was nice enough to notice that I had lost a few bowling balls. She told me that Al (who was at work) was still on the diet but was not a fanatic about it. In fact, she said he cheated a little here and there but had not gained much weight as a result of it.

We had to tour the house as both Teri and I liked Kay's furnishing and decorating ideas. So with 6,000 square feet of living space to look over, we went eagerly through the house. We walked into room after room admiring each one. Al's office was built with deep rich cherry wood through-out making it like a library or an attorney's waiting room.

The pool outside was professionally taken care of as was the manicured lawn and shrubbery.

We did so much talking that before you know it Al showed up and the first thing he wanted to know was how many weeks or months we were staying. I know that he was kidding, but we actually enjoyed ourselves so much that I am certain that a part of him would have liked to see us stay for at least a few weeks.

Terri and I feel that to enjoy friends to the fullest we do as much as we can in a short period of time. We have a tremendous amount of fun and leave on a very high note.

We enjoy gambling so without a thought we went to Tunica, Mississippi. It was like a tiny Vegas. We had a wonderful time, gambling, eating catfish and ribs.

We had to leave, but we told Al and Kay we would visit then again on our way back from Florida. So we took off for Chattanooga to visit my old Mack buddy Chuck. He had a home on a lake in Georgia and we wanted to see each other. On the way there we saw the ranch and home of the country singer, Loretta Lynn. I had no idea how massive the facility was—everything from horseback riding, camping, motocross—not to mention her impressive home and museum.

We got to Chuck's vacation home and it was like nothing I could have imagined. The view from Chuck's house was something that you would see in a magazine and the value of this home had to be at the million dollar mark. It is nice to see your close friends do well but deep in my heart I was saying to myself "Franco, what the hell happened to you?" Fortunately, both Chuck and Al are not the type to throw something in your face. To the contrary, they downplay their wealth as nothing more than mere luck.

It amazed me that Chuck was still in good shape and was as good at telling stories and as generous as ever. We stayed briefly and told Chuck to please come and see us in Phoenix to spend more time with us.

Going through Atlanta is always exciting for me, as I truly enjoyed it when I was living there. I stopped at Atlanta Raceway to see the statue of Richard Petty and other drivers that I admired. We bought a number of items for the grandchildren and proceeded to Sebring racetrack on the way to visit Teri's cousin in West Palm Beach. Sebring is really different from Atlanta. It has a road track with so much history that celebrates my favorite automobile, the Ferrari.

We finally arrived in West Palm and since Teri had not seen her cousin Chris for nearly ten years we enjoyed ourselves immensely. We had now come almost six thousand miles and so I had the Infiniti serviced at the local dealer. I played golf with Chris at the Breakers, a very fancy club. We played a good game of golf.

After leaving there Teri and I went to see my mother-in-law, Mom, with whom I still kept in close touch. Mom lived in Port St. Lucie, Florida, not very far from Chris. So we visited Mom and she was as sweet as she could be. I brought her tapes so she could see how the family was coming along. We had a nice cup of tea and we admired her cute little spotless home. Our intention was not to stay long, as we wanted to get to Fort Myers to see my long time buddy Gerald Hausman. We had gone to grade school and high school together and I first met him fifty years ago. We had started to become reacquainted on the internet. Gerry lived with his wife Lorry on a Florida gulf island near Fort Myers.

On the way over to the West Coast we stopped in Naples at an Italian restaurant chain called Buca di Beppo. We had been in the one in San Francisco as well as the few new ones in the Phoenix area and we enjoyed eating there. Normally we don't go to chains when we travel as we like to try new things but something attracted us to go there. I think we were ready for a very nice secure meal. Ordering for me even with my diet has not been difficult. I order items like calamari and then go to a salad. The service and food was excellent. Our waiter was a nice young man of about twenty-five.

I told him, "I used to play hide and seek in that coliseum," pointing to the painting hanging on the wall. "That was before I came to America to live in New Jersey."

He said, "I was born in New Jersey."

"Where in New Jersey?" I asked.

"Oh, a small town, you've never heard of it," he responded.

"Try me," I said.

"Berkeley Heights."

Trying not to look surprised I said, "Did you go to Columbia School?"

He looked puzzled, and said, "Yes!"

"Did you go to Governor Livingston High School?" He was open-mouthed by now. So I went on. "Remember the Little Flower Church near Columbia school and that little old lady that had her pizza joint just past the school and Delia's Liquor Store?"

We laughed and I told him that I had spent a very important time in my life growing up in the same town he did. I left him a big tip that he deserved.

We managed to find the Hausmans' home on Pine Island. We found ourselves in front of a two-story home that was surrounded by acres of beautiful landscaping. Once past the gate we got out of the car and I hugged Gerry for the first time in over forty years. He still had that same smile. He was as glad to see me as I was to see him. Lorry and Teri became acquainted quickly while Gerry and I went off on some crazy stories.

We finally settled down after a dozen wild memories and decided that we would stay for a day or so. We had a lot to talk about. In fact we talked right through the afternoon and into the evening, and then into the early hours of the morning.

You never know what impression other people have of you. It's easy to see how they affected you, but I had no idea how my life had influenced Gerry. Here I had been always a little envious of his former life and the relationship he had with his family. And now he was telling me that he had never forgotten the times he came over to my house for one of those big Sunday dinners. He remembered my mother and my grandmother and how gracious they were to him, and he had really admired my brother Aldo. I suppose we all have a tendency to like another person's life or situation. We imagine they have it better than we do. This is especially true when you are young.

Anyway, Teri and I enjoyed Gerry and Lorry's lovely home and their two huge Great Danes. They also had a hot dog—a dachshund. There was also a parrot that talked extremely well and turned out to be a super watchdog as nothing got by him. Lastly, they had two cats who were always fending off the dogs.

The back of the home had sliding glass doors that opened on a bright blue pool. This was all screened to protect you from the bugs.

We were given the entire upstairs, which opened onto a very large deck that overlooked their private pond filled with lily pads. You only see these sights in magazines and yet we had been fortunate enough to have slept in three places that were so beautiful. And the best part is that we had been there with our friends. America is pretty great.

After breakfast the next morning, it didn't take us long to start telling stories again. Gerry and Lorry are themselves storytellers and writers, and that is how they make their living. I was proud of that, as I had known Gerry "back when" and he and his brother Sid were always writing and drawing and making music.

I found out now that Gerry had written fifty books and that with his wife, they had actually done another ten. They spent a part of each year visiting schools talking to students about how you can make a living at writing.

We had a great time and I think it was much easier for Lorry to understand the crazy friend that Gerry had talked about all these years. Anyway, we went out for dinner on another little island, and then Gerry threw me a curve.

He had now heard the stories of my entire life and he said that I must write a book about my life. "Few people have lived so many lives in one," he said.

I chuckled and said, "Who would have any interest in my life let alone to purchase a book to read it?"

He acted surprised. "Everybody has a story to tell, but in your case the story is worth telling because you came over here with sausages stuffed in your pants and now you're a millionaire, and you did it all through hard work. What story is more American than that? It's the American dream. The difference is that you could actually inspire people to try it for themselves. Your story doesn't end in abject misery. You may have a garage full of Ferraris and Zimmers and antique Mercedes Benzes, but you haven't lost your appetite for fun. You love life. Couldn't you put that message into your life story?"

I had never, to be honest, thought of my life as anything special—except for the helping hands I have had over the years, the angels, if you will. But other than that, I think I have lived a pretty normal life. But when I thought about how many times I had come this close to death, maybe that in itself, might make an interesting book. Gerry seemed to think so, too. "Those near death experiences, those would make quite a story, along with how you came up from poverty and tried to become the president of Mack Trucks. But, mostly, it's the journey of a family man, and people are going to relate to that."

"But how should I write it?"

He smiled and said, "Just tell it. Don't tie yourself down and try to write it as if it were a terrible chore. Just talk to yourself or to Teri, and the story will unfold."

Those words stuck with me as we wound our way home to Arizona.

We headed north toward Panama City as that had a tremendous amount of memories for the Antonetti family. I relived some of those memories when Bette Ann and I took the children to the beach and they were collecting sand dollars. Actually this was the very beach where Buddy got such awful sunburn when he was about ten years old. I remembered how we used to break vitamin

E pills and spread the oil on his skin to make sure that the scars would go away. But there are still some scars even to this day.

We had another great fish dinner that night. In the morning we called Kay and Al to let them know that we would be in Biloxi Thursday morning. They decided to meet us wherever we chose.

So when we arrived in Biloxi, we went around and found a place called the Sun Tan Motel. It was one of those older motels, clean and spread out on a single floor, and with parking in front of your room. We got a very special deal and that was that. We were happy and as soon as we got into our room, we started to unpack for our three-night stay.

Finally Al and Kay arrived and our fun began. We were all like school kids joking around. I told people at a restaurant that they were lucky that we came there, as Al was a famous writer and he had recently been at the White House. Al acted shy and Kate was hysterical, and people were trying to get Al's autograph.

One early morning we had breakfast at the Waffle House. We had played all night and also had eaten at this incredibly beautiful restaurant and here we were six or seven hours later in a Waffle House. But we were again in a very silly mood and as we conversed, I referred to Al as a hit man, and again Kay was losing it while Teri was afraid we were going to get locked up. Everybody in the restaurant looked at us suspiciously, and I went on about Al's skills.

So we played, shopped, ate, and gambled. Monday came and we followed each other to Jackson, and then Al and Kay drove on to Memphis. We then headed on to Roswell, New Mexico, hoping we might get beamed up for a short while—that would certainly give us something bizarre to talk about at the next Waffle House.

We stayed at Eagle Guest Motel in Roswell and scouted the town and learned a lot of funny stories regarding the UFOs and how the tourists have saved this town.

There were only 4,000 people before the UFO incident occurred, and now the town was over 40,000 people, and the Roswell Space Museum was selling "artifacts" all day.

We drove by White Sands Missile range as well as the Astronomy Observatory. There were great dishes placed all over a ten-mile area like massive eyes and ears, looking and listening to outer space.

When we came close to the Arizona border we were met with heavy smoke from yet another forest fire. We needed rain as there had not been any for months, and the ground and the trees were dry. Without the rain, the beetles were eating up the forests, and the cycle of destruction was at hand. One little spark and everything went up in smoke, as it was doing now.

We now were close to home but my gut feeling told me that I had to go slightly out of the way and stop at the Indian casino in Globe for one last fling before returning to Gilbert. We did okay in that one hour stop, picking up an extra $65.00. We were home by the evening of July 15th. We had been gone 34 days and traveled over 9,000 miles. We had seen a lot of history and shared a lot of memorable experiences with our friends.

Alas, my son did not take care of our fish pond, so we lost many fish because the filter had not been serviced. I went to Home Depot to buy another pump, and on the way I forgave Buddy this small lapse in duty, and went on with my life.

The following day it came back to me what Gerry had asked me to do: "Write your book." Not knowing where to start, I just began and after a number of hours into it, I started enjoying it. I sent Gerry the first eight pages of my life and I asked him to be candid with me—was it any good? Did it make sense? He encouraged me to continue saying he liked it and it was worth the effort.

I have been on this project since July 17th my birthday, and it has been an obsession, trying to remember everything exactly as it happened to me fifty years ago.

I have done the best recollection that I am capable of; maybe some things are out of order slightly, but that is the way they came to me, and, in any case, I was truthful.

One thing occurs to me now, and it is this: I do believe that I have been gifted with knowing a number of extraordinary people. Such friends, in today's world, are extremely hard to find.

As for my family, I know that I have wonderful children. I am very proud of them and I love them dearly.

As for my marriages, I truly loved my wife Bette Ann as she was my sweetheart and she was taken away at a time when she was not her true self, which saddens me. But we did have nineteen years together, and we shared two lovely children that she brought into this world. My second marriage was a mistake, but it gave me a son, and I know I will be with him sometime soon.

I was given a second chance in finding a wonderful woman in Teri and her children. The affection I have for her is true and we enjoy one another and share in our everyday activities without ever saying, "you should do this and I will do that." We just do whatever needs to be done.

Love, I believe, is different as you grow older. So I cannot compare the love for one or for another, but I can say that my void is being filled by Teri, and for that I am thankful.

I sincerely hope that anyone who reads my story will receive some value from it, and if that is the case, the hours that I have invested in this endeavor have been well worth it.

Anyway, FIFTY-NINE YEARS OLD AND STILL ALIVE!

Biography

Franco Antonetti is an American-Italian born in 1944, who, as he states "loves this country as much as his next breath." Educated in Italy and New Jersey, Mr. Antonetti dreamed of becoming a success in the world of trucks and trucking. His extraordinary rise at Mack and his co-ownership of one of the best forklift companies in the US was meteoric. However, he insists that his desire was really to "live in the greatest country on earth and to have a family." Today, he is retired, and when he is not doing things for his grandchildren, he writes and tells stories, something he learned to do very early in life. Mr. Antonetti is married and lives in Gilbert, Arizona.